# THE BLOG
## THAT BECAME A
# BOOK

EDWARD TRICE

Writers' Branding
1800-608-6550
www.writersbranding.com
orders@writersbranding.com

# The War in Iraq...

April 23rd, 2008

There must be something yet unknown in this sequence of connected events. How is it that we, as fellow humans, can sit idly by while being insulted with the lies and hypocrisy that that seems to flow unabated and unending from our government?

Five years ago, this administration ordered my country's military forces to attack Iraq.... The mission.... : to capture a terrorist,... to find and remove "Weapons of Mass Destruction"... to rid the free world of a potential nuclear menace....

None of this was ever a truth and there was never a capture of this terrorist...

This is what that action has spawned:

- The death of over ten million Iraqi citizens

- The death of over four thousand American military members

- The loss/cost of over one trillion dollars

- The permission of genocide, crimes against humanity in Sudan, Darfur

- The neglect and decay of our schools, health care, infrastructure

- The absence of the National Guard and their material support

- The absence of desire or effort to respond to natural national disasters

- The mismanagement and pillaging of our national economy...

- The destruction and erosion of respect for our country at home and abroad...

I do not understand why these issues are not a prime priority every day. Issues that are noticed and addressed until accounted for and remedied by all of us, especially our elected leaders.

What am I not knowing?... Can we just be sitting and condoning liars, thieves and murderers   serial liars, thieves without conscience, and mass murderers all with unquestioned and undeniable guilt, take our freedom and all our future heartfelt hopes and dreams away....?

# Our lives at risk

May 29th, 2008

I disagree with my government on a number of things. Some of them I cannot begin to justify or see the value in their actions at all.

The issues that stick in my mind above all are fathered by capital punishment. It is not a solution for justice to anyone. It does not deter murder or atrocities against mankind. War is an atrocity: planned murder on a mass scale.

Capital punishment always is another... murder—a homicide that is planned and sometimes celebrated. How can that ever be a deterrence? The only deterrence for killing is not killing. There are other options for eliminating vermin. There are ways we can isolate and maintain control of threats. We cannot redeem our pain and suffering as victims. Does capital punishment help that? How does perpetuating killing make us feel better?

Every life has a right to live, and in those lives lay the salvation and hopes for the better life, growth, and even to the extension of our collective human life to include our personal joys and pleasures.

If capital punishment helps at all, would it be as gratifying as knowing that you are not a killer or a partner in taking life? Taking a life deprives humanity of that individual's gifts or purpose to help us live. Could our accomplishments possibly have been increased or enhanced if so many humans have not been murdered? Is War "mass capital punishment"? Is War a cruel and inhumane game played by effete and selfish men that never ever were good for all? Surely, it is without any worth except to remind of us of how stupid and heartless we can be. How many innocent victims die simply because we accept killing?

We must resolve to support and even cherish all life with a clear emphasis on human life at every opportunity because it is our life that we are.... saving

# The Election

August 27th, 2008

The presidential election of 2008 has become the most significant election in the history of the United States.

The incumbent Republican administration is a growing dysfunctional embarrassment at every level. Beginning with the election of 2000 and the crimes that were committed to deny an honest result, to staging an unjust conflict that has cost the country it's best citizens, best soldiers, balanced economy, world respect at every turn.

To have a woman as a candidate was a shocking first. To see her lose to an African American man in the primaries was stunning at every primary. The thought that racist America could have a "Black" president has defied sanity... and it has yet to happen but this candidate is intelligent, honest, and above all organized and supported...

This present administration has also defied sanity and has been so destructive to the American values, ideals, and everyday fabric of the country that the unthinkable has become a sensible option to all, even the bigots and racists and elitist are revolted by the lack of purpose, integrity of this group of thieves and war criminals.

The rest of the world is almost glowing with the hope and change that this candidate promises... Maybe America is really a beginning of all the best in governments, the leader in human freedoms and the cornerstone of all humanity existing in a growing peace, harmony and purpose for everyone

Posted in Health, Politics, Sports | No Comments »

# The Election... after the shock

August 27th, 2008

When the campaign began in 2007 for the next president and the administration that he would be representing... the war was an atrocity and crime against humanity, the economy was an ongoing scam that was failing miserably in every way; the general health of mankind was obviously neglected and deliberately mismanaged for the profit of private interests. The abuse of power, and callous disregard for all humans especially the poor, the minorities, was evident beyond any denial.

The incumbent administration and their elected leaders and representatives were gross in their guilt and their lack of any integrity. This had set the stage for a complete although overwhelmingly late reforming adjustment to truth, and self-respect.

The shock of the results of the primaries paralyzed me. The fear of the continuance of atrocities and horror that would have been at the very least placed in another human's hands was only relaxed by the fact that that different human would be a woman....for the first time. She was defeated.

I am certainly not above being wrong but I am no longer as naive as I was... The result is ominous. Since the primaries they have attacked Obama in every way that was not a possibility for Hillary Clinton. Personal, snide, cynical racist comments and innuendos have prevailed and distracted the focus.

The point is that, this is not about any person per se or a popularity contest. This election is about issues and injustices that has affected the world, the country, the neighborhood, the individual for longest of measured time. The fact that this time this administration has been so irresponsible, so arrogant, so racist, greedy. inhuman in so many ways, without any doubt and above all with no conscience or regret in any way has provided a perfect opportunity to clean the slate.

They have provided a list of continuing facts that are not at all vague or unclear:

- The War in Iraq and the lies to justify it
- The rape and pillage and atrocities that followed
- Abu Gharib
- Katrina
- Poverty in this country and contribution to poverty in underdeveloped nations
- Corrupt officials... Halliburton
- Economic failure

These are just the known issues. These are the dangers to our future that can be addressed and stopped. These are the stakes in this election. These are the subjects that should be held in priority at every opportunity. The perpetrators, yes, perpetrators, should be held accountable.

Posted in Local, National, Politics, Social Interests, World | No Comments »

# I will not forget

September 11th, 2008

This is the Republican Party of John McCain.

The flag carrier for George W. Bush, Dick Cheney, Donald Rumsfeld, and John Ashcroft. These men have left the party without any dignity or respect. They could not show their face at their own convention. They are guilty of misleading my government, my fellow Americans with their lies, greed and mass murder.

This has never been acceptable and they were so arrogant and so ruthless that they could not be mistaken or separated from it... These vile people could not find a candidate that was reasonably clean after disqualifying Giuliani, Hucklebee, and Romney. All guilty by association and support of that dastardly crew.

Enter John McCain, Lt. Cmdr, not Commander, not Admiral who spent his war service as a POW. An honorable man who has no history of thinking independently, he chose under pressure, an obscure woman governor from the least populated state with very little traceable history or experience. It reeked of a totally transparent attempt to pander and seduce the women of the United States. Could this be their only possible plan?

A plan to steal the election with racism as their cloak and personal petty distractions as their weapons. I will not forget that this is a historic election not because of an African American being eligible or a woman being on the ticket but because of the madness that has gone amok. Madness that can be trapped and eradicated by honest citizens who are tired and no longer blinded by the obvious attempts to distract focus.

America is a microcosm of all that humans bring to this planet... Dreams and despair, astounding success and crushing failure. All humans and conditions are here. For two hundred and thirty years it has existed with the growing potential to fulfill a national government's best standard.

Now all the vermin and their ilk and their acts are exposed. Their acts are undeniable, their intent without question, their lack of decency or respect for humanity openly emphasized daily.

I will not forget this election provides an opportunity to clean house... It is a fight, a true battle between haves and have not. No punches are held back in a battle or fight such as this. There is nothing to gain by holding back. Poor and middle-class whites and blacks see that they have been victimized. There is no reason to listen to liars and prevaricators with a history of continuing their insults through some distorted irrelevant rhetoric. Their sons and fathers and, yes, daughters have died in Iraq. They have been denied access to education and health, to say nothing of quality of life. A trillion dollars misspent if not stolen. Halliburton needs... serious attention too.

This is not personal although it can be felt by every person. The gloves should be off. This is a fight to correct the wrongs of mankind at this moment and in the right arena... my country, The United States of America....

I will not forget.... I will not. forget.

Posted in Politics | No Comments »

# Interesting Times

June 14th, 2010

It has been a while since my last post. Many events have happened. The natural phenomena earthquakes, floods, volcanic ash all have surely occurred before. The elected leader of the most significant nation on the planet, an African-American, is a stunning first. Certainly to me.

It began with the defeat of Hillary Clinton, at least my being stunned did. As her defeats mounted or as Barack Obama began winning, I thought it was some diabolical plot by the opposition to make it more possible for McCain-Palin to win. No, I could not see, dared not think that an African American male could be elected president of the United States, the Leader of the free world? That was not even a joke at that point. Then it happened.

Barack Obama won the election.

In the eighteen months of his administration, I have seen and felt the wave of relief and hope for the future that simply was not there before now. His courage, his heart is always visible and he can think and talk clearly about what he is thinking and doing... too!

It was a bit much at one time don't you think? Anyway, he, this Mr. President, proceeded to stop the economy from a dead fall, this included keeping banks and financial institutions/industries from collapse... all against republican adversity, lies, and nuisance obstacles.

Iraq, a dastardly, embarrassing page in US history forever, is almost free of US service men deaths.

A depression, not recession, escape by his initiatives all with complete opposition from the republicans... Good thing they lost in 2006 but don't remind them... So, he and the weak-kneed Democrats had to do it by their selves.

In eighteen months, a definite positive change in social and economic climate except for the hate mongering right wing radicals and conservative microscopic minds that controlled the pathetic past president, who some say, may have been... "challenged" all his simple life. They seem to be more visible and totally unapologetic about their deviant behavior.

The Health Care initiative or bill is not only a necessary asset to all Americans, it has been prepared, detailed and accounted for since the first draft. To the agony of all that are in need and would benefit immediately... waiting,... after unbelievable opposition by the same usual suspects, the lame ass democrats managed to pass it...They need to be taken to the shed at least, Mr. President for general principles.

But that is another thing for later... I see an obvious pattern here.

It seems that the GOP, Republican party, conservatives, Tea Party people does not want anything to pass from this administration or be accepted. These same people who were voting for McCain, the War, and all the horrible Bush administration actions. Actions so abominable in every way mentionable that they made the possibility to vote for an African American  much easier. He won by capturing 70% of the first time voters... amongst other things....

The problem for all this administration's "Ills" can be addressed immediately and effectively by holding the perpetrators, better known as the Republican Party accountable. Well, Oil leak in the Gulf is really big and not included. in these simple house cleaning problems

Yes, I said "house cleaning."

These are the same people who voted for Bush, Cheney, Ashcroft (remember him?). They lost a monumental election in '2006 that enabled this change to take roots. If they had controlled Congress that time none of what followed could have ever been possible. They lost in '06 because the people had enough of their lies, self-serving greed and inhumanity to mankind. Even though they lost they still did not get the message and that will be part of their next lesson but for now....

Enough is enough.

Criminals, War Criminals, traitors, perjurers, should all be brought to justice, whatever the aftermath. Progress will be impossible if we permit them to escape accountability. All congressmen who were supportive of their shameless efforts should be exposed and held accountable.

The Criminals first and foremost because they stole my country, my country's moral respect and honor while continuing to perpetrate lies by killing innocent humans on a staggering scale.

If you give Eric Holder permission to start the "house cleaning" they, the "Republicans" will be so glad that Health Care passed, will love education and infrastructure initiatives... might even find a way to plug that oil leak. But more importantly, they will know they are accountable for their words and deeds... at last.

Posted in National, Politics, Social Interests, World | No Comments »

# Oil Spill

June 21st, 2010

First, I like Mr. President, Barack Obama. Why, you ask?

It seems to me that all the problems in this administration's tenure are being addressed and taken care of. A sensible clear approach with consideration for everyone involved seems to be the plan... without a prepared script.

This oil spill is a disaster of epic proportions. It is a shock and horror on all living creatures including mankind, especially in this gulf region. Mr. Obama insists on "hands on" direction. He then chooses responsible competent people to lead, to solve and apply solutions as his delegates.

In this case, what is truly significant is holding BP accountable and, being responsible, powering in a factor to more than compensate for the financial loss, cost and retribution to impacted families and business.

It cannot be any better.

The leak will be plugged at some point or capped. The clean-up will be done.

Over a period of time the Eco/environmental loss will be rehabilitated and reestablished all under BP's commitment to pay for all them. All? Yes, ALL.

They did it and they will pay for it. This is the best part. MONEY from BP to immediately help sustain and to ensure that the victims, people and other life forms won't be suffering... too long.

Compensation for the victims....sounds like a "won" case in US, civil court with the trial being held already and...well, you understand where I am going.

This Mr. President is a professional legal advocate for the people. Final estimates and figures have yet to be noted but twenty billion dollars out of the gate is not a bad start. It could be major depending on what follows. This could change the future of the whole south in a very positive way ultimately.

Ironic, this dour, sad, scary moment being the dawn of a new beginning, a brighter day forever... for the South.

Posted in News | No Comments »

# My Giants

October 3rd, 2010

It hurts to talk about the Giants because it is my only team.

I love sports but the Giants make it infinitely more personal. Suffering through their losses over the years and getting silly happy over their wins was all good as we say today, but the stench rising from the camp now makes it hard to breathe. I have smelled it before coming out of Jacksonville awhile back. Then it was burning my nose hair before they hired Steve Spagnola from the Eagles to save their last Super season.

In between that odor offended many people, players in particular. Great athletes quit the game because they could not play and gag at the same time, Tiki Barber, Mike Strahan for two. Of course, it contributed to injuries and loss of players through other residual effects that tossing your goodies could easily be connected to.

It has become a dark day as of late because the malodorous aroma has been totally difficult to ignore, except by brown nosing friends and bigoted press.

To be blunt, the coach, Tom Coughlin, is probably a good person, caring parent and family member, this is speculation, absolutely is "clueless" as football coach and that is the source of that overwhelming odor that surrounds my team.

Who else would expose an injured player, Aaron Ross off of rehab to the kamikaze special teams on his first game back? Who else would risk their franchise quarterback to injury again and again with idiotic transparent play calling? But, for the icing on the cake, keep his best runner, a true cannon on the bench. A player every other team in the league would commit an assault to get if they did not have to pay some penalty. A player who is being paid 25 million dollars to sit. He has done this before. He inflated another player to the detriment of his other players, owners, fans and thus producing a losing season,... and caused serious injuries to the "Cannonball "Brandon Jacobs and others by calling the wrong running plays and strategies. Oh, the inflated player is. Derrick Ward who is.  I don't know where he is now but he got paid thanks to "Clueless Tom."

If this seems personal about Tom Coughlin, it is! I think I said that before.

In conclusion, I always want the Giants to win and I have been wrong before. There are so many other "incidentals" it would seem a bit "bitchy" of me to whine on.

The Chicago Bears, today's opponent, are good test. Ironically the Giants had a choice of Coach Lovie Smith when they chose Tom Coughlin. The Giants have great players, a legendary young GM in Jerry Reese. I hope for their sake Tomtom doesn't take any one else with him when he goes.

Posted in Social Interests, Sports | No Comments »

# Oil Spill. Revisited

October 3rd, 2010

The great Oil Spill of 2010 has been successfully plugged. That wasn't something that could continue, much to the dismay of the Obama haters.

Yes, it is sealed but more importantly, the victims are reaping the prospect of a new beginning thanks to this President's diligence foresight and planning. No cost to the tax payer. In fact, the money is being monitored and delivered on a timely and needed basis. Unprecedented in our annals to my knowledge.

There is more "good" news. The worst recession since the Second World War has been declared ended. That deserves some thought. We are talking 65 years here. The economy is stable and on the growth side. Wall Street is smiling again or maybe for the first time in a long time too. Jobs are in the want ads again and are being taken. US autos are gaining respect as they begin to thrive anew.

The dour, depressing, criminal days of the last administration are no longer in the weather predictions. Except for the decimated remnants of the terminally polluted Republican party. The Tea Party, the Conservatives, so called religious rightists, are now exposed and the only common threads are their unmitigated racism, yes, I said it, bigotry, and stupidity seasoned with perversion brewing in a pot of inhumanity.

Which brings me to the solution to that... problem.

I am not totally happy with our President. He has yet to hold the perpetrators of the greatest crimes in the history of mankind accountable. Liars, murderers, crimes against humanity, thieves of the heart and soul of our personal self, and of our purpose of our nation. They are still active although guilty many times over. Conviction would be a given if he only would say to AG Eric Holder, "Take care of this business next."

Yes, it might be the end of "old times" for some, certainly would clean a lot of trash out of the streets, while cleaning the environment a bit too. It also would complete his promise to us, and the world at large, to end the atrocities of the last administration. He certainly has to be accountable for his actions, why shouldn't they?

Posted in National, News, Politics, World | No Comments »

# Epitaph.... 2010 Giants

January 4th, 2011

The odor that persists of the now "deceased"2010 NY Giants comes not only from their reluctance to fire or remove or retire their clueless coach. No, there is an extra here.

A GM who has yet to be heard from.

Or why would ownership be speaking when a GM who happens to be a genius at picking drafts and replacement is still in office?

This coach, Clueless Tom Coughlin, was never Jerry Reese's, the GM's Choice. Legend has it that Wellington Mara thought Coughlin deserved a shot. A shot is seven years with a miracle and the following casualties, four defensive coordinators, multiple players, fans, loyal fans, team spirit and self-esteem/respect....

Jerry Reese was Wellington's choice too, and Ernie Ecorse's too... How about giving... Jerry Reese a shot....

Let the GM choose his coach like the other GM's in the league do.... Giants

Posted in Sports | No Comments »

# Excruciating times times....

December 21st, 2010

This crushing lost was delivered by the Eagles. It was not a surprise. This loss was agonizingly slow in its development. Every game had elements of this loss exhibited by the ineptitude of the coach to coordinate his players and their efforts to be supportive or be in harmony. The power of an offensive running game, time control and management were most glaring.

All season the coach of the New York Giants was Tom Coughlin." He has misused and abused players, and this classically upright sports organization with his lack of ability to understand or to try to work with his assistants. He is stubborn beyond belief and the Giants paid big time yesterday.

Eli Manning is not Michael Vick but he is a great athlete and quarterback. Brandon Jacobs, Antrell Rolle, Kenny Phillips and above all Perry Fewell deserve better.

There is no one else who would attempt to pass the ball with a 21-point lead in the last 8 minutes of the fourth quarter when he has runners like Brandon or the misused Ahmad Bradshaw, no one else. This "coach" causes injuries to innocent hard-working athletes daily. He adds insult to injury by blaming others, i.e., Matt Dodge. The general manager, Jerry Reese, who has supplied the team year after year with the best drafts, and supplemental emergency players in the NFL has to endure perplexing decisions like placing Vincent Cruz on IR for an emergency kicker replacement. And countless, over the years, other agonizing decisions by this coach. Yes, Tom Coughlin and only Tom Coughlin is the problem. The game on Sunday left no question unanswered about his lack of ability at any level to coach.

There is only one solution to this "hot mess." Fire Coughlin, dismiss Coughlin ASAP. Before he takes others down with him....

Oh yes, the game yesterday... horrific from a Giant fan's point of view... but, then again, Michael Vick is a great athlete and the last thing he needs is time to play, which "Clueless Tom" provided over and again with his choice of plays and wrong players in the wrong positions at the wrong time… Perry Fewell and his defense couldn't overcome these setbacks. Jerry Reese and the Giants fans and organization deserve better.

There are better coaches available…. The time is now….

# The Last Election

January 8th, 2011

The remnants of what was called the Republican Party has claimed new victories in the election in November 2010.

The party that was shredded by their own incompetence. The party of that previous administration now says they have new life. The "Tea Party" seems to be the password among these people. Their hottest conversation is spawned by topics from the "birthers," or "repeal of the health bill."

Nothing.... about losing a half of a billion dollars in aid for one state's education system or another quarter of a billion in aid for an overwhelming needed mass transit tunnel after one year in office in that same state.

Nothing about "Iraq," Enron, or Halliburton.

Unfortunately..., for them, they refuse to face the truth. Like many of us, they need help,.... serious intervention.

These Republicans were obstacles to all the successful initiatives of the present administration. They were supporters and conspirators in the previous disgraceful decisions of the past. They have yet to account for their lies, crimes, and human atrocities, okay, "political misdeeds" in the last administration. They are racists without shame.

The truth is since they so poetically prepared the 2008 election for the victory of Barack Obama and his being in office for two years.... change has become evident...

The economy has been rescued from free fall.

Financial Institutions are stable and have governors to monitor their practices.

Disasters have been handled with confidence and efficiency.

The Auto industry in the US has been resuscitated after flat lining... A health care package for all has been passed...

War deaths have been drastically reduced...

A restoration of trust, belief, and pride in being an "American"...

They, the Republicans or now, Tea Party, or Conservative Party, still has "no candidate"... They scurry and shake the same old bags finding the same old vacuous and superficial phonies... George Bush was their best!

That is all history now, and soon... they will be too.

History harbors a lot of human ills that were overcome or erased.

This past election is largely a result of Obama not holding the perpetrators of past misdeeds accountable. Some people need to be brought to justice. NOW...

As we see, their "winning" the past election brought their old habits to the front immediately... Reneging on campaign promises and stuffing their pockets.....

One week in office....

Eric Holder must be given the directive to bring the liars, perjurers, murderers, criminals of the past administration to justice. Cleanse the air.

This cannot be ignored much longer because these people need THAT kind of help...

We need that help toomore than they do.

Posted in National, Politics, World | No Comments »

# A New Year.... Old Tragedy

January 20th, 2011


For the New Year or any year, the horrific act that played out in Tucson, Arizona last week is shocking, threatening and heartfelt by most all I know. The most disturbing fact about that incident to me is that it is "familiar." Not new in any way.

The victims change. They are the famous and the infamous, the children and the aged, family and people whose names we cannot pronounce at all. All of us are still exposed and vulnerable to senseless catastrophic violence. Yes, I say, murder, even singular is a catastrophe for all of us. People kill other people. Suicide is a downer too even if the mortality rate is only one.

Since the earliest times, this option to choose life or death has been exercised with the choice of weapon(s), or motive, offered like appetizers at a banquet. Do they really make a difference? The main course is "Death," to someone or more than one. That is always another tragedy when over...

Then where do we get to feel better.? When can we put this "accepted behavior" behind us. We as human beings who wish to live and live unafraid must choose not to kill.  for any reason. Even murderers should be free from being killed when brought to justice. Yes, capital punishment is useless in preventing killing. It actually perpetuates the act by a planned, deliberate, public display of killing.

This humane act is not a new concept in any way but. It must be the only way. Countries and governments that have abolished "killing" or capital punishment have so much less of these  old tragedies

Posted in Local, National, News, World | No Comments »

# Catastrophe.... in Japan

March 15th, 2011

Words do nothing to describe the event that has mushroomed in Japan. The pictures take your words away. The thought of potential future ripple effects push beyond your worst nightmares or imaginings.

The reality is not to be escaped or denied. We are human and even in our safest abode, totally vulnerable, to say nothing of our mortal destiny.

That said, then," what else is there"?

There is still the precious blessing of living now, of having still the opportunity to ensure and commit ourselves as a family of humanity, regardless of our terrestrial boundaries, and our different cultures, skin color, or petty differences and goals.

Committing ourselves to helping each other without limitations, to the preservation of all life at all costs.

To stop killing each other and start saving each other.

Yes, we can still do that. We have that choice in front of us.

Coming together to choose tools and methods to do this should be simple, easy, if we remain dedicated to our goal.

Feuds and reasons for not caring and not helping all humans to a better existence seem so trivial and worthless in contrast.

To preserve the only jewel in our treasure which is LIVING, being alive to enjoy that short period to which we all must eventually surrender,. that is all we have.

Posted in Health, National, Social Interests, World | No Comments »

# The State of the Union....In Reflection....

March 28th, 2011

First of all, many things were not mentioned in the "speech "at all. The issues that were bemoaned by Republicans, and disgruntled Democrats, man in the street and the downtrodden, as avoided or omitted do have untold importance.

However, these same issues are all dwarfed by the success and accomplishments of this administration.

This is now what the" State of the Union" really is.

The economy rescue from complete collapse continues to heal and grow strong

War and its casualties.... subsiding...

US Auto Industry resuscitated

Health Care Reform

Unemployment on the decline

Successes and Tragedies handled with competence and a sense of dignity and respect.

Exposure of the racist right wing and its costume called the Republican Party. These critics from the Tea Party, Conservative Party, and turn-coat opportunistic Democrats are the same flakes that supported the criminal administration that preceded this major change.

They are truly still the only obstacles to progress. Yes, these slow learners and self-righteous naysayers persist and slow advancement down in every way they can. They cannot stop it, however, and whether they know or accept it, change, in its inevitable way, has set in.

Change is reflected in the diplomacy with other nations, in the rise of democratic passion around the globe.. Without rattling sabers this administration has charted a sane course through the minefield of international diplomacy.

An economic and political rapport with China

A nuclear Arms treaty with Russia

The US does not need to show its muscle to prove it has strength or resolution...

Change, a different time we are living in....

Posted in National, Politics, World | No Comments »

# A Daddy Day

March 28th, 2011

It was one of those portrait Spring days... Late afternoon, birds singing freely now, Sun on the slow setting, flowers blooming so strong their fragrance wafting up to the second-floor bedroom window.

Yes, spring was in the air and The Daddy was lying in his bedroom listening to his music, smoking his favorite pipe. Things couldn't be much better, he was thinking. The mortgage payment was made, shopping had been completed and the lawn and grounds were manicured. Relaxing was the moment when he heard the shrill shriek of his.... daughter, Sonde'.  the baby girl.

She was the youngest, not a baby any more but Daddy's girl forever, you know?

At best she was ten or eleven, but her shriek was a bit ungodly... Not the usual in any way... Dad jumped to the floor, pipe still in hand and an extra heartbeat or two for the jitters and met the Sonde at the door.

"Dad, Dad" she was saying... " A dog, a monster dog" was terrorizing the neighborhood "and had chased her and her friends with the threat of chewing each one up on the spot. "He is on our lawn," she said...

Dad breathed a sigh of relief A dog. All that noise and calamity about a dog? That was a bit much he asked her. She said, "No, Daddy this dog was different."

As she started to explain her fears about this.dog,    Dad    decided it would be more expedient to go downstairs and take care of this "emergency."

He walked outside on the step plateau of entry, into the bright yet setting sun and looked down.... as he heard a most unearthly growl... The sunlight was blinding so he walked down the steps to see where this rumble was coming from. He saw... a oversize malamute/husky/ wolf-like animal, very big, the more he looked, turning on his lawn to face him. Dad's first thought was to get back into his house, his safe house... but the dog deliberately blocked the way. Now Dad's heart was beating very fast and as he backed away the dog was meeting his eyes with that fixed stare. Dad stared back but now his thoughts had changed.

This was not going good was one thought... This could very well be a life changing moment... not the thoughts he felt good having. He watched the animal eye to eye. The dog's growl seemed to get deeper and louder  Then eye to eye. This dog took a long piss on Dad's newly manicured lawn!

No, he didn't do that... deliberately was one thought but... yes, he did...deliberate or not. Dad had retreated to the sidewalk now. All the neighbors were viewing, from a safe distance. The dog was on the sidewalk now too. Dad asked his baby son to go get his hickory Stick. A 6ft.long 3in. circumference stick that he kept for situations that got out of hand. This clearly was one of those  Man-man, that was the baby boy's pet name, went to get it. He brought back an old moping handle. Not Dad's keepsake in any way and tossed it to his father. Dad was shocked but this was not a time of many options. He'd rather hit this, "foaming now at the mouth animal" across the back than have his ass chewed up in front of the world and be embarrassed and wounded for eternity. "Damn "how did I get into this fix. was his thinking.

Dad's lawn was on a raised plateau with a very nice brick wall around it. the wall was high but the dog was walking in front, still eye to eye with Dad. Dad decided to strike first and he did. He swung the mop handle to cut the dog in half. A loud snap followed and Dad was now holding a 2ft broken mop handle stick. It broke on the wall which was a fraction higher than devil dog's back.

Ooooh, the chills went through Dad now. The dog seemed to sense that something had changed and Dad could see he didn't like that stick that broke on the wall at all. Now, my turn he seemed to be grinning. Dad was in too deep to run now for sure. So, he kept eye to eye contact with his predator. Dad cocked his broken stick like a miniature baseball bat and waited.

He could feel the animal's muscles tensing, he watched the dog's eyes.... the dog leaped... at Dad's head or neck or face... but he was met in mid-flight by Dad's mighty stick... right in his open mouth. The blow spun the animal around in flight and when he landed, he was bleeding, profusely, moaning and howling instead of growling. He limped off... leaving Dad in one of his most triumphant moments.

He saved his daughter... hmm, the neighborhood, maybe but he surely saved himself.... What a day....

A real Daddy's day....

A true story....

Posted in News, Parenting, Social Interests | No Comments »

# .... Celebration of Change... third year in the making....

April 27th, 2011

This year is seemingly charged with a series of actions and events that continuously stuns the senses.

The most interesting phenomenon to me is the implied existence of the "Republican" party.... which, is supposed to spawn a candidate to oppose the "Democrat" incumbent... I linked them both with amused speculation at best and this is why.

They no longer have the disguise, or ability to avoid being seen for what they truly are.

They are the party that has an overwhelming void in decent, consistent, responsible, caring and above all, thinking representatives.

Politics in itself has an odor but it is a necessary stench as a side product of the mixing of the individuals. Then, there are those that have a clear scent of their very own that they bring to the arena that is decidedly unpleasant. This is not any relief from other bad smells ever. The Republicans cannot stand the odor of each other since the election of an African-American.

They do not know what to say in public.

The clichés and bumper sticker phrases are an insult to everyone in its short life span.

The Tea party faction was a party (no pun intended) joke which never was quite in the humor zone of most republicans.

The conservatives cannot unite on what issue is primary or secondary for that matter.

The religious right and the "birthers" are equally pathetic...

These, Ladies and Gentlemen, are the Republicans...!!

The President has yet to remind them that they voted for and supported the leaders of the last administration. The names of those leaders gag me a bit because I do not know why this President hasn't held those past "leaders" or at least some of them accountable for their lies, murders, conspiracies and criminal deeds.

Maybe, he is saving it for "new" campaign ammo. That would be a convenient time that the timing couldn't complained about.

So now the "Republican" party is reduced to a trillionaire as the leading candidate. A trillionaire in bankruptcies is more accurate. This familiar face is "worn" by the man who is their leading vote getting prospect. No extra ammo needed here.

It amazes me that their own decimation seems to evade their awareness. Perhaps, this same blindness and lack of reality accounts for all their past crimes and injustices rationalized or dismissed as insignificant or worse, never occurring.

This "Republican Party," all of them, are as good as done. Unless they can return to a time where racism, elitism, nepotism human injustices are accepted. That thinking never was really acceptable. The illusion is not possible any more.

Posted in National, News, Politics, Social Interests, World | No Comments »

# Japan.... continued

April 27th, 2011

The events following the catastrophic earthquake lend much to the imagination. One does not have to wonder about the effects of the tsunami that followed. The disaster was on every picture posted around the world. Videos will be testimony for ages to come.

The nuclear reactor meltdown that followed is an ominous prospect for all who can read. The containment and prevention of a continued or progressive calamity poses an endless problem. A very real threat to all mankind forever...

"Is that possible" we ask... over and again. The answer comes only in our thoughts. It is too final to state or face and address. openly, democratically on the world stage.

Searching to assign blame is as much a waste of time as ever although that exercise is repeated over and over.

Chernobyl was a lower level of incompetence or was it? Nuclear waste is an inevitable byproduct of the industry. No one designed or planned a "safe" method of disposal. What?! How can that be possible? It is possible.

Initially, the nuclear question was probed and developed as a weapon... to kill. I am sure there were other purposes in the grand scheme of planning and use but I remember bombs, an "Atomic, Hydrogen". andother titles that spelled doom in untold numbers as an achievement. This reeks of the worst irony, doesn't it?

Now, the unspeakable is have "we" (we are all here together if the water currents and air currents collaborate) slipped off the edge? Are "we" so close to Japan?. Is my cat going to eat the wrong sushi and who knows? This is a very small vehicle we all share as a space station, our Earth.

It is not at all too late to help others!

Japan needs help immediately.

We will be helping ourselves in that process.

It would also be an immediate help to commit to the preservation of all life,

The respect and compassion for all life, as soon as possible.

Vow to help all other humans to be alive and well.... We still have time for that...

Posted in National, News, Social Interests, World | No Comments »

# Egypt.... an inevitable... Libya . . . another story

April 27th, 2011

The change from Hosni Mubarak to a new administration is long overdue... Now that the change is a reality the trend is to link it to some specific political agenda. An agenda that has been identified and categorized if I may use that broadly.

The reality is that it does represent a change in government, in the heart of that turmoil called the "Middle East."

The murky details coincide with the recent murky history of new administrations in that area of our planet. Libya was following suit or change was being introduced there too. That change is a work in slower progress due to a more resistant and brutally decisive leader, Moamar QuaDahfi. Ruthless is another credit attributed to him often.

The most common events in both of these ongoing changes are the increased death toll and the statistical fact that most of the victims, fatalities are Muslim in faith. Islam being the national religion means they are killing each other  Killing and maiming each other.

A civil war of some sort, that would suggest but with a curious abundance of outside participators, interests, and goals.

Freedom for the masses, Control of the Oil, Taliban, Palestine and Israel at risk.

Then again, a closer view reveals that all that has really changed here were the excuses and rationale to justify the mass murder and other inhumanity to mankind that is impossible to hide....

Just knowing these acts are taking place offends me. Hearing about it, with skin color, religion, social economic status as a "stipulation" of some sort to separate it from our personal lives or justify the toll is insanity to me... I can easily resist that loss of my mind.

To be continued....

Posted in National, World | No Comments »

# Dayenu.... A Mother's Day Salute

April 27th, 2011

I was born an only child. I think that's what helped my early years to be lonely. Toys or imaginary friends were not enough. Having many cousins did help but only when we were together. That was on Sundays. We all went to the same church every Sunday, even Sunday school before church.

My Mom was the family flag carrier when it came to church or serving the lord, as she sometimes put it. She always had a Bible, or an assignment to accomplish for the congregation. She was always ready to distribute the message word. So, Church was her base. This did not help my need for company in any way.

The word "friend "always was and is still a most significant word to me. I wanted to be a "friend" and to have them.

What was and still is a friend to me? Well, my Mom was my first friend...

A friend begins with another life to share mine with. My time, loyalty, companionship, fun, were always a primary part of this format. As I gained friends, I started to define the word in more personal detail.

Girls became my preferred gender choice. No arguments or petty disputes. The earliest games were "Doctor and Nurse," or "Mommy and Daddy". That was a really good one.

Girls, women, ladies were always the top or primary to me. My Dad was very cool but my Mom was. Mom.

Grandma? There was nothing like her in the whole world to me. So, I grew to appreciate and to value women. Early in my life This didn't take anything from Grand Pop. Like Dad, it was not an issue to compare. That was just the way things were.

I realized early the separations that religion and ethnic cultures appeared to make. They seemed to contradict the concept of "human family" at times.

Being raised a "Christian, or Protestant, or Baptist," seemed to make it easier for me to be curious about girls of the Hebrew faith. I really liked to read and as a child, the Bible was one of the few books in our house.

Eventually, I met the spirit of Eve, Esther and Ruth Judith.

Their names were now Jeri, Christine, Libby, Arlene, Margaret, Marcia, Sandra and Joan, Carmela and certainly Theodora, all of whom I am eternally thankful for.

These women chose to provide me with umbrellas and parachutes. They shared the subtleties of being aware, of being respected and understood.

Yes, some were lovers in the most literal sense but surely, I felt love from these women in every sense, as I did from my family. My need for friends was clearly enriched by these women who chose to be teachers and guides in this journey of my life.

My friendship needs continued to expand and the fulfillment of my needs stretched beyond national, social, economic borders. I have been blessed by all women.

However, to make this all enough, my greatest blessings from women came from those I have never met. They are the keepers of all outside of my needs that makes all life worth living. They bring all life into existence. Mothers, wives, sisters and daughters, they are the protectors and nurturers of all men and children.

I am eternally grateful for the other human being, Woman, for she is the caretakers of all or everything that exists.

# The Presidency... His accomplishments and disappointments

June 22nd, 2011

On the threshold of the next campaign in 2012 we find ourselves assessing the past elections. Not only the last major in 2008 but all of the local minor elections too, if you want to be honest and thorough.

New efforts must be retooled again because of the reluctance to accept progress and change by the Republican Party. The remnants of that group would be more accurate.

The successes or accomplishments are not at all as complete as this critic would like. The primary reasons for this are that some patterns are long term, a different approach to a lifelong issue. The disappointments are more available and easier to determine so we will begin there:

The first is a lack of effort to hold the perpetrators of the crimes against humanity and our constitutional laws accountable.

This last administration was an abomination. The lies to steal from our government began before 9-11. The attempts to control our rights, freedom of speech and other freedoms were constant. The electoral process itself was manipulated in more than one state.

Lies under oath, lies to conceal crimes were pervasive. It sunk corporations. It destroyed our economy and definitely caused the death of lives, families, hopes and dreams. This is still ongoing as much as possible because NO ONE has been brought to justice... or held accountable.

Then there is the war on Iraq, the atrocities inflicted on captured prisoners and the innocent citizens of Iraq, the soldiers and their families that were serving their country and erased, and the pillage and plunder of a respected ancient culture, all unlawful acts in sequence that continued unabated until the election of a "not possible" candidate.

All efforts to bring change or to progress from this dastardly base has been blocked, refused and politically manipulated by the same den of low life, yes, they are still busy at work... Why has this been permitted? What happened to an investigation or inquiry to determine accountability?

Secondly, the "New Jobs "to be created from an effort to repair or strengthen the infrastructure has yet to emerge. What is that about? What happened to new highways or rebuilt highways, bridges and safety measures, hospitals, and schools. Nothing is visible on that front to me.

I suspect both are linked to the same solution. To be specific, this rag-tag group of bigots, racists and pseudo-Christians, conservative, tea party gang bangers formerly known as the Republican party need a gardener. Accountability would weed out the vermin that perpetuates the contamination of the best of that group and certainly would give everyone a chance for progress.

Accomplishments. Wow, just the continued air of progress is undeniable.

The Healthcare Bill.

The end of the Disgrace in Iraq.

The rescue of the economy from another Republican produced depression.

The rescue of the Auto Industry.

The rescue of Major corporations, especially Banks and Financial institutions.

The routing of Al-Qaeda and resolution of Osama Bin Laden. The withdrawal of our forces in Afghanistan with Iraq surely to follow.

Keeping his campaign promises... not all, due to the Republican efforts to thwart his every initiative   but the tally is clear.

The exposure of the Republican Party... for example... Candidates for 2012? Giuliani. he knows better or running for any office is out of the question Pawlenty.... Romney.... Palin. ? It gets worse!

Governor Christie of New Jersey! The same person who cost the state over 750 million dollars before he could find a seat that fit his profile. The Federal funds for education and Federal funds for a most needed "tunnel" have been sabotaged. The loss to the children of New Jersey and the commuter /worker in the tri-state region cannot be calculated. Broad based attacks on unions and specifically the teachers are cruel and actually demented. This is what is left of the GOP after the election and successes of Barack Obama.

Most importantly, he managed the return of worldwide respect for my country and its deeds and purpose that was in consistent decline with both Bush administrations. He has chosen a cabinet, made Supreme court appointments that have proven their worth and credibility while presiding over a most significant period in our national and world history.

Posted in Local, National, News, Politics, World | No Comments »

# The Giants... and NFL Football

June 28th, 2011

When are the Giants going to let Jerry Reese play his cards? The changes that have occurred has brought the Giants and the league closer to understanding the difficulties in player negotiations only.

There is nothing that helps the Giants with The Tom Coughlin problem. Yes, there is a new assistant special teams coach. The draft choices will need to prove themselves and I have much confidence in that based on Mr. Reese's past choices.

To risk the season, Eli Manning's career, Brandon Jacobs and Ahmad Bradshaw, the brilliant young receiver corps, the offensive line with the same lack of creative decisions that are the choices of this head coach bode a sack of continuing problems for the team and their legendary loyal fans.

Like the rest of the world, we must wait and see what happens. While waiting we will remember that this coach is not the general manager's choice and nothing but a Super Bowl victory this year should prolong his stay.

Posted in Sports | No Comments »

# The War on Drugs.... 55 years of lies and morbidity

June 28th, 2011

Wars always have casualties. They are the price of the victory if you can lose your feelings to comment. What happens when you have no victories only casualties?

1956 was back in the day as the saying goes. Someone chose that year to attack the illegal drug trade with a declaration of War. The enemy was the user/addict and his suppliers. All connectors to the same people or their network were also declared "enemies" in this War. The victory would be in the elimination of illegal drugs and the punishment of the users and the suppliers.

This elimination has not happened, although the punishment has been so cruel and damning for the convicted that they become pariahs forever. In fact, the opposite has been the rule or reality. Users of illegal drugs have multiplied. The number of vendors or suppliers are beyond counting. The deaths and destruction of users, law enforcement officers and families of all are also more than can be counted. There is much to be acknowledged in this dilemma.

First is the beginning. It was not 1956 actually. The attempts to prohibit and criminalize the use of illegal drugs came in the thirties. It has become another exercise in futility that followed the failure to prohibit alcohol. The ATF, FBI, IRS, state and local police could not stop people from drinking alcohol, booze, moonshine. They could not prevent major influences and prominent families from transporting the best that could be made or obtained. The tools and efforts of the government could not keep alcohol from their appointed designations or people who wanted to consume it. It has been offered that those lettered bureaus had no reason to exist after failing or being ineffective so they chose to attack marijuana use, cocaine use and branched out as the illegal drugs differed and grew.

New laws were created as older laws were intensified by compounding the consequences.

The legal drug companies supported this effort in every way they could, understandably.

These "companies" are predators in their own special way. They employ and support lobbies to influence our elected leaders. The leaders are woefully unable to think for themselves except to ensure their reelection by any means.

All too often, their "means' supports insane punishment for this health problem of addiction. It is further enhanced by the need of exaggeration to implement fear in the general public. This act which is carried out in police procedures, correction enforcement and incarceration perpetuates the status quo. It is a continuing series that goes further away from solving any problems.

It creates disrespect for police and authority due to coercion, bribes and futility at gaining any solution. It creates an exploding population of prisoners and ex-convicts whose lives are destroyed. Their families are innocent victims forever. The sickening stories of these lives torn and shredded by these continuing lies and distortions to keep the "business of drug control" are a travesty of justice and an atrocity to all mankind.

The platform is fueled often by right-wing dementia and conservative racism. There is perhaps and an endless array of supporting factors but to say a victory in the war on drugs will happen is a sad fallacy.

There can be only one victory in this war and that will come through sane and compassionate legalization, like in Las Vegas Gambling or Prostitution. I deliberately picked Las Vegas because of the extreme application of both activities. It is working and has for a long time. Taxes help in many ways due to the popularity of the sources. In Amsterdam a prototype exists daily. Monitoring "users" or addicts is an easy task with results that are measurable.

The "crimes" of the cartels and the profits of legal drug companies will decline... Some people may never go to prison so the police can concentrate on the sick serial killers and a multitude of other sociopathic profiles. Liquor and cigarette companies might take a hit too.

I think the ongoing charade is much worse and with no end in sight it is senseless to continue in this morbid act of depravity. We can still be humans with compassion and good will to each other. It is not too late.

Posted in Health, Local, National, News, Politics, World | No Comments »

# Our Lives at Risk II. /the Death of Osama Bin Laden

June 28th, 2011

The war is still raging. Iraq is seemingly more quiet now. Afghanistan, a Waterloo for the Russians, has led to the Pakistan network that eventually uncovered Osama Bin Laden.

Yes, the same one that had eluded western attempts to be captured. He who defied international efforts at all levels to be captured for ten years and was assigned the responsibility for global terror. The same one that masterminded the horror of "9-11? That one.

His contributions as a living human was ended with a bullet in his head. Good riddance to bad rubbish some said. Celebrations occurred. That seems to be the preferred formula. , to kill. Everywhere. Bullets from guns, suicide bombers and the murders of children by family and friends all continue unabated. I've heard "if it works don't fix it." That is the problem. Bullets and killing doesn't work, that is, if the goal is a peaceful nourishing existence for mankind.

Obviously, that isn't the goal then. If that isn't, what is the goal. Are we all in line to get our ticket to some planned elimination! Life in its "beautiful journey" has plenty of pitfalls and tragedies without that planned end for some obscure and trivial excuse. That's the real war that rages on. Killing each other. In a subway, or in the schools, the home or the streets of our homes... Capital punishment. I ask again, "Are we safe yet?"

Osama was the ultimate terror threat. Did killing him make you feel safer? We all agree if anyone had to go he was the one? The after effect of ridding the world of so much potential misery should have brought colossal relief. It did not. Nor has the death of his lieutenants or aids. His death gave the victim's survivors... Revenge... Pay back. ! For what? The agony forever that the families of the victims must endure? Not in a million years! It did authorize the immediate killing of others for revenge... pay back. The wrenching anguish of the supposed pursuit of Bin Laden and his Al-Qaeda /Taliban comrades while leaving wounded and dead all over the planet was a travesty and a horrible waste of human life and dreams of families around the globe. Has killing him freed us from the threat of being killed? Not yet, it seems to me. It certainly hasn't affected the killing in the Middle East, in the schools, in the homes and in the streets at all. I still see some attempts to glamorize and justify these absolute ultimate crimes. The war rages on. Because we have chosen to kill. By any means necessary and for any reason.

Strangely, the only rationale that is untried is "TO PRESERVE AND DEFEND THE RIGHT TO LIVE." At all levels, gun or weapon controls are must. War games must cease. Dialogue and acceptance of our human kindred is mandatory to begin to achieve our goals. Respect for our individual religions and life choices make sense to me too.

All of that would begin the process to eliminate the risk of our lives being threatened.

Posted in Local, National, News, Politics, World | No Comments »

# Our Lives at Risk.... lll/... Norway

July 28th, 2011

.... The killing continues...

The excuses for condoning or accepting killing are all pointless. The fact that this measure of atrocity has been carried out by one singular individual is the issue. A collective understanding of this act or discussion only increases the morbidity.

For any reason all of us are still at risk because we the people of our small planet earth are quiet or mute about these acts. We have yet to embrace as a united group, the fact that all life is most important.

This deranged pathetic human has no purpose except to make it crystal clear that taking life only perpetuates more lives to be taken.

Of course, the solution is not immediate and there may be a long line of deaths before the causalities start to subside. It certainly isn't any help to "kill" this low life... Again, no remedy in revenge or satisfaction either.

Now if there were some preventive measures in place such as collective efforts to restrict arms, or weapons of destruction, not mass only, and more importantly a joint effort by "governments" from the national level to the village level, by religious factions to social factions to not condone or support the taking of life it would at some point minimize these acts or the opportunity to initiate them so freely.

Yes, this is really long-range thinking and perhaps some dreams are easier to support or believe have possibility. The absolute fact is that continuing as we have is not at all acceptable. Norway is not the Far East, the Balkans, Africa or the streets of the United States. The change in locality of these insane purposeful acts does not matter. The results are the same.

So, I am to believe that that is what humans do? Some humans do? Certainly, the masses or majority of humans do not. I don't and won't.

I am excluding an instance of immediate self-defense that takes my desire to survive such an attack to that unwanted conclusion. There are many others like me, perhaps the majority in this case without a doubt, or it would be worse, if you can imagine that.

No, I am not that kind of peaceful person... I want to live. I want my family and brethren, all humans to live. To live without this constant threat from anywhere for any reason

We all must start somewhere and the sooner we start the sooner we will approach a pattern of eliminating risking our lives.

There is much too done, on a broad scale, for a seemingly endless time into the future but that does not mean we should not begin that journey...

We must emphasize at every level that all life is equally important to preserve and respect. Surely, some people need to be separated from society for the safety and well-being of... society. We can do that easier and with a healthier and freer conscience and example than by killing these individuals.

Their hate rhetoric must be argued against and their movements once confirmed need monitoring. We do that now just not at large and collectively. We cannot be hypocrites in these measures. This may be the most difficult of all mandates because we, as humans, each seem to harbor hypocrisy at some level or many levels.

Nevertheless, we must continue, persevere if we must, and push through all obstacles to ensure the preservation and the protection of life. That may be our mission now, since the humans before us were so limited in all the ways we, as humans, are not limited anymore...

Posted in Local, National, News, Politics, World | No Comments »

# The Republicans... again/ the Debt Debate

July 28th, 2011

Mr. President,

When are you going to take care of the business at hand? How can you let these sick miserable excuses for leaders continue to obstruct human progress? Please note... HUMAN PROGRESS. . .! So, this is democracy at work?

The new elected leaders, neophytes all seem to be digging a complete hole for the sake of refuting you Mr. President. The conservatives are gleeful, gleeful while the rest of us loyal Americans cringe and squirm. They are counting on the public being so unnerved and frustrated that your reelection will be in peril?

I do doubt that it will be enough... America will not forget the lies and crimes committed at random by the last administration... They cannot take any credit for ending the atrocities in Iraq and Afghanistan. They alone brought this country into a depression unparalled in history. They did bring the government to a halt under the Clinton administration with one Newt (the contender) Gingrich in the front. They would do anything to get you and your progressive administration out of their way. Unfortunately, they have yet to realize that they no longer exist as before. This is 2011 and their covers have been removed. The truth is there for all who may seek to know. A new day is in progress. Thankfully.

They fought your Health Insurance and caused it to be a skeleton. They stole the surplus in the national economy. They erased/stole/ misappropriated it all before 9/11. During that time, it was in the black 212 billion dollars with the idea of being out of debt by 2012 under the "Democrat "Wm. Clinton.

They totally ruined human relations with fellow Americans and foreign entities. Friend and foe. Their decency and ability to think are proven to be self-serving at best, at the risk of all others. Obviously, I see no reason to harbor their demented excuses for not agreeing to a budget.

So why not just arrest the culprits that lied and stole and convinced the former president to spend without measure on Wars and personal pleasures. Where did the rich get the idea that they couldn't be taxed? Why isn't this issue being made clear in more detail?

I must say your courage and your determination to persist is impressive. Your hesitation to bring justice and complete the clean up on the core of sick and criminal leaders is not.

It is suspect because I know and the world knows justice would put a stop to their continuing nonsense. It would eliminate the rest of the garbage that festers and provides food for the "tea party" and the "new" members in the house. Please give Eric Holder, the attorney general, permission to launch inquiry or better yet an investigation on the issues that were rampant when you surprised the world with being elected.

This Republican Party is on life support at best... They finished themselves with internal cannibalism and disgusting greed. They have written their epitaph with lies, confusion and hatred. Their attempts to find an opponent for you is a sad farce.

Please get on this and let the chips fall where they may...

Posted in Health, Local, National, News, Parenting, Politics, World | No Comments »

# My Giants

August 18th, 2011

The 2011 New York Giants are preparing for another Super Bowl run. I suppose the other NFL teams are having the same goals as they also prepare.

It seems that all the experts are discounting the Giants. Opinions aside; this is what sport fans do. The most popular reasons for not seeing the Giants winning lies in losses through free agency and a lack of free agent acquisitions. If I had to pick a weakness it would still be the decisions of Coach Tom Coughlin but that will be put aside for now.

The GM, Jerry Reese, has weathered criticism since he began his role in 2007. They did win that year, thanks to a special defense brought in by Steve Spagnola. Tom Coughlin is moaning about the losses in free agency. I moan about his inability to use play-action offense or running the unique backs provided by the GM and throwing to the excellent corps of wide receivers. Mario Manningham, Hakeem Nicks and the totally unused, due to Coach putting him on IR last year, Victor Cruz. The Giant's losses in free agency are part of the structure of free agency. Plaxico Burress, a great receiver, does not deserve any more than he was offered and refused by the Giants. He took the money. I do not fault him, best wishes, in fact. Kevin Boss is a good tight end. Thirty-five catches don't raise many eyebrows as a season total. He also took his best offer.

The Giants are loaded and here is why. GM Jerry Reese knows football and what is potentially a good football player. The league is seasoned with ex-Giants that were cut by the Giants or took better offers from teams salivating to get them. Reese's draft choices are wanted all over the league. Brandon Jacobs was one of his first. Ahmad Bradshaw and the mentioned receiver corps, offensive line, refurbished on the move. The defense wreaks of his choices clearly and if not forced to defend a short field by the ill offense decisions by Tom Coughlin, are the most physical and capable in the league. Yes, I said it and it is a fact. They can and will defend a short field too.

The secondary is very good and seasoned. The defensive ends, Justin Tuck, Osi Umenyiora, if he signs... and the Baby Monster Jason Pierre-Paul are great athletes, super strong and fast. All kinds of mixes can be made at linebacker The draft was a success as usual for Jerry Reese.

Our vulnerability lies in Coughlin being reluctant to adapt or change his approach to almost everything. After looking at his face duringthe preseason opener last night. It seems his face reflected severe constipation or something similar. Oh, and no play-action of the type any other coach would love to force down an opponent's throat.

Sit back Giant fans, this is preseason. We will have good season if our vulnerability is addressed. Just that one.

Cannot wait till it starts.... My Giants.

To be continued....

Posted in Social Interests, Sports | No Comments »

# The Workings of Democracy— America the Beautiful

August 18th, 2011

This is the chosen nation, The United States of America. There are so many "confirming" factors that I will find it difficult to touch all in any way so we will have to settle for the few that linger in my thoughts.

First, we have the broadest and most diverse population. It is a unique collective. There are those that choose to be here, immigrants and their descendants, native born and a kidnapped people who have stayed after freedom and multiplied. Then there are the incarcerated population, three million strong by last count.

It, our country, is founded on freedoms. Speech jumps to the front for me. Freedom of the press and the freedom of choice. This is to choose our leaders and our personal goals and lifestyles.

We are fortunate here in America, truly fortunate. With such an abundance we must not neglect our responsibilities. One mandatory responsibility is ownership of our actions and deeds. Our country is a relatively young nation, two hundred thirty-five years old. Many other nations have more years with that distinction. They do not have the threads and fabric that is forming the garment of America. It would appear loosely that many from all walks and nations came here to blend and form what will be the image of all that our planet contains.

In this country and perhaps, more than any other country, one can witness the graphic demonstrations of democracy at work. The changes in leadership without the overwhelming fury of discord resulting in bloodshed and masses of humanity disenfranchised in this transition. At least, on the surface it appears that way.

The economy, jobs and living conditions to be more specific to me, are vulnerable to the relationship between our elected leaders and the people who elect them. It must also be said that the relationship within their brotherhood as elected officials has a determining result on the success and failure of "the economy, namely jobs and living conditions."

The battles that are a part of our country's design will continue. Our ownership of the past deeds and the people we elected has set the table for the present meal. That meal consists of a sincere effort to eradicate racism, nepotism, and the hypocrisy of equality and justice for all.

We have moved dramatically forward in the election of 2008. The abominable performance of the prior administration cannot be ignored or left unaccounted for. This administration had to end an unjust war, save the auto industry, rescue the financial institutions and provide a healthcare system for the impoverished and have not populace. These conditions did not just appear in that last administration but they were egregiously implemented then. The sacrifices of all Americans were at peril until the people chose to live up to the ideals and purpose in our constitution and in the hearts and conscience of our humanity... That was clearly a new beginning. A major step forward on the path of all humans being valued and respected for their content, there is no going back!

Posted in Local, National, News, Politics, World | No Comments »

# The Workings of Democracy.... America the Beautiful ll

August 23rd, 2011

As we citizens progress to the next election we can definitely see some shape taking form. Listing the accomplishments of this administration is not being noted or addressed. The efforts of the opposition are clearly to fault at every turn or opportunity anything possible.

The past Republican administration is not referenced or mentioned. The officials and leaders of that administration are lying low very much like criminals in hiding. They are an embarrassment to the pretenders of new choices. Their acts and their crimes are still not addressed or even accounted for. They are still there, lurking in the closet like the rest of America's dark past.

Yes, a great country we have in this United States, but like human beings, this country of ours is not perfect. The Republicans are not the only problem individuals we have here. This is not just a party issue. This is a people problem.

America has substance and the format to be all that is promised for the good of all mankind. This is not an instant fix or overnight possibility. The dark past is rooted in long time injustice and abuse and disenfranchisement to many people. It was inflicted by the founding fathers and continued at random until the present. The founding fathers were just "people" too. So, hatred, racism, genocide, sordid lies are all part of America's historical past.

Presented under many veils, a mere sincere focus and thought reveals the truth. Unfortunately, because these dark passages and distortions are unaddressed and not thoroughly erased, they continue, under different veils and other disguises. They are clothed in distractions, petty neighborhood arguments just enough to keep one off the true problem. They have different vendors, Rick Perry, Sarah Palin, "the Tea Party," Michelle Bachman.

It can be "the Economy" but not their record on such. It can be foreign policy but theirs was always war. It can be social relations, for them that was separate and forever unequal. America grew in 2008.

It appears over time the distortions and the truth have been hard to separate. This is not to play the "race" card or to cry "victim." It is just simply the truth and we all are victims until it is accounted for and erased.

This present administration has been denied legitimacy until that absurdity couldn't last and then every attempt to make any accord has been obstructed and compromised. America has not embraced progress. It has been forced on my wonderful country by time and the higher conscience of humanity. These petty squabbles over anything are really excellent propaganda. In fact, the media of today makes Joseph Goebbles, the media director of Nazi Germany, look like an amateur.

In summary and conclusion....

This Republican Party persists in spite of truth and past performance. This President persists and provides truth and consistent performance.

We can start with the economy... or can we? Where were these Republicans when the Bush administration was going amok?

China... joining other nations to sanction Iran for Nuclear responsibilities.

Passing the first Health Care Comprehensive Act in U.S. history in spite of incredible obstacles continuously by this other "party."

Persuading or enlisting Russia in limiting the growth of nuclear weapons

The auto industry on solid footing and PAYING back government subsidies.

Rescuing the financial institutions from total collapse.

Closing the issue of Osama Bin Laden.

Libya and other despotic regimes collapsing with our effective sensitive diplomacy.

The proposal of the most massive job initiative since the last great depression has already been obstructed by the elected conservatives, "Tea Party"and assorted mental misfits that now scramble for position in the "Republican" party. It is to the credit of the portly Governor Christie that he has thus far resisted joining the fray.

Is this really America? Yes, it is! Working to be better and struggling to overcome its weaknesses, my country goes forth in the democratic process of setting the standards for the world to live by.

Change is inevitable. It was very obvious in November 2008

# My Giants... continued

August 30th, 2011

Here we are with the second preseason game of 2011. No one has addressed the decisions of Coach Coughlin. He is immune to scrutiny? Why?

Eli Manning makes his calls based on the coach's plan. Being an avid fan only, I am curious how it is supposed to confuse or baffle the opponent about your next play when you have no runners in the back field. Does this telegraph "PASS" here? In this day with behemoth linemen and attacking raging linebackers how is he, the QB, supposed to get the play off. Without getting killed or mauled or both. No disguise or subtle misdirection at all. Terrible Tom Coughlin almost had a casualty per game of every season! Can we count that!

Eli's interception rate is directly related to these things. Tom Brady has Belichick watching his back. Belichick doesn't have any runners at all compared to the Giants or players like the players GM Reese has provided. He does employ his runners and players to their strengths as opposed to some cramped dream that never worked and is blown up before the players get off their blocks. How the defense is supposed to rest or defend errors made continuously by offense mismanagement. Why is everyone being criticized but Tom?

History tells me he has never had a good quarterback. Please think about that! He is a quarterback's worst nightmare that's why.

History tells me he has never won and has been saved by his defensive coordinators and miracles. He has alienated his players since he was hired on any team. He has played his favorites rather than the best player or their best options.

More importantly, Eli Manning and Jerry Reese have had only him for their head coach. Why should they be at risk for his bonehead errors? Why should their careers and the careers of the rest of the team be subject to this consistent stupidity?

Seven years of excuses and constipation is what Tom has brought us. What does he have against Brandon Jacobs? What other coach would put Victor Cruz on kamikaze detail? Danny Ware over Jacobs in substitute for Ahmad Bradshaw? He did the same thing with the long-gone Derrick Ward, a retread with the Jets, who thankfully went somewhere else and rapidly wore out his welcome.

This coach creates problems for his team. His opponents laugh, and wait until he helps his team self-destruct. It is time to look at the coach of the Giants. Coaches can be replaced a lot easier than a gifted player... especially when they are their own worst enemy.

Posted in National, News, Politics, Social Interests, Sports, World | No Comments »

# The Resurrection of the Giants.... 2011

September 2nd, 2011

Before the season begins, there is only one thing that must be done. The coach, Tom "Constipated" Coughlin must be relieved. of his duties as coach if nothing else or the Giants remain dead.

The Giants have won and existed lately because of the draft choices and free agents of the GM, Jerry Reese. This is glaringly obvious. Tom Coughlin's regime has eliminated players for every reason imaginable. He seems to specialize in personal injuries and disillusionment of their personal goals and self.

He has never been the choice of this general manager. The players of the last seven years have been victims of his failures. This will continue until he is gone.

This not fair to anyone, not even Tom Coughlin. He must be better suited for something else. Surely, this is not his best comfort zone. His face throughout the games reflects confusion, pain, and disgust of player efforts, his player's efforts!

He always faults his players or some other factor, weather, league rules anything other than his ill choices and inflexibility.

IIis misuse of Eli Manning, Brandon Jacobs borders on criminal and is constantly insulting and demeaning. He has alienated players from the beginning of coaching and winning titles has not happened except for Steve Spagnola saving the 2007 season.

He is totally incompetent and he must go ASAP for the security of his team's health if not potential victory.

This is the only coach, again, whose very face constantly reflects the lack of control and capability needed to direct a group of any sort, much less an NFL football team. I do not know what he knows but it is not players, or effective use of players, self-control, or how to teach players. He, again, is constantly blaming his players for mistakes and bad judgment, yet he is responsible for their learning. A COACH TEACHES!

If that, teaching, is the problem he is an abysmal failure.

The problems, if he is kept, are much more difficult to remedy and maybe will have lasting effects for decades....

Posted in Local, National, News, Politics, Social Interests, Sports, World | No Comments »

# Our lives at Risk... The Necessary Closure

September 2nd, 2011

There is no reason to prolong the investigations required to guarantee the abolition of the lies and manipulations of the freedoms and human rights that were abused by the Bush administration.

We have all suffered. The people who did these dastardly crimes are still active and their format is being supported. It is an insult to justice and the integrity of the country that this has not been addressed. Some arrogance is so pervasive that books are being written to cleanse their abominable acts.

The deaths of American soldiers, the deaths of humans from Iraq and from other countries around the globe all cry out for accountability. The loss of trillions of dollars, the manipulations of elections and other crimes to numerous to list must be addressed and accounted for.

This may be a sordid task to carry out and may take a while to complete. It is, nevertheless, absolutely essential to begin. Like "housecleaning," a long time coming, but when it is done all the inhabitants feel better. Starting the process is the duty, now, not a minute later.

Our justice system is at risk to say nothing of more lives. The poor excuses for obstructing progress and the delays that have followed are a direct result of these criminals and their crimes not being confronted and accounted for.

When is the attorney general going to get the assignment, he was born to do, Mr. President? When are we going to be free of these threats to our very existence at every level? Why must we wait any longer? I, for one, would like to know...

Posted in Local, National, News, Politics, World | No Comments »

# The Sisters.... Williams

September 10th, 2011

It seems a mere short moment ago they were playing tennis, both teenagers. Hair locked braided with colorful beads in adornment. Venus and Serena Williams, beautiful, lithe, fluid grace in motion. One was tall and so fast it seemed she was everywhere on the court before the ball got there while seemingly quietly competitive and politely crunching the ball with each stroke. The other, nostrils flaring, fiercely smashing that tennis ball with each swing as if she wanted to reduce it to powder. Shorter and more muscular she bellowed on each swing like a martial artist's blow. Both were a joy and wonder to see and victorious to monotony.

Loving tennis as I do, the joy was personal all the time. I am sure other fans had their reasons to be interested beyond the ordinary too. They certainly were colorful. They were magnetic on and off the court. Their "Dad," Richard, was with them always and knew them better than they knew self. He brought them to the top, unconventionally and against all odds.

That was then. Time does take its place and toll on everything, especially all life. Some "things" live longer than others. Trees and reptiles seem to approach mortality denial but humans are mortal and the sisters Williams are very human.

I have seen in my time many "humans." The sports celebrities seem to be most known. Entertainers, film stars certainly seem to reach worldly recognition but sports figures take on super human images almost god-like, if you can relate to a "God."

They, the sisters, took time from their peak tennis years to pursue other personal dreams. We missed them right away. We needed them in our tennis dreams like no other recently. They were so good.

Now, as always, time waits for no one. The ladies came back but it was a different day and the struggles to be fit and consistent presented new obstacles. Venus withdrew from the US open today after having serial setbacks with fewer triumphs. Serena battles on but the domination of yesterday is not totally apparent yet and if it does it will be short lived. Time will not permit it.

I, for one, will miss them with every tennis match. We won't see the likes of either again or least for a long time. I will remember the joys and excitement they generated and be forever thankful to have witnessed such beauty, grace, and power in a fellow human being always.

Posted in News, Parenting, Politics, Social Interests, Sports, Uncategorized, World | No Comments »

# Nine Eleven....plus Ten

September 10th, 2011

This is another day that will never ever be forgotten. We all have these days but this one will ring loudly because of collective factors that touch all humanity.

The ability to tune in and witness the catastrophe unfold in our very presence adds to the impact and makes a mark on our psyche like none other. To be a spectator at the mass murder of thousands of people will always boggle the mind.

There has been more death in a day, more in the flash of an instant but the slow-motion effect of the two planes striking and the collapse of the two largest buildings in the world will always be staggering.

The war against Al-Qaeda was not the first choice. In fact, the choice of Iraq as the perpetrator was a total lie and more innocent people were killed, murdered, slaughtered.

This, to me, is the real common ground. People deliberately killing other people. These were not soldiers or military was the lament. Neither were the citizens of Hioshima on August 6 or Nagasaki on August 9. Those two days were justified by saying more lives would have been lost if my country hadn't dropped their only two, at the time, A-Bombs on Japan. There is no justification for this.

This is another day that will never be forgotten.

Can anything ever remove the pain, the hurt, the forever gone future of the deceased? Is the eternal memorial as a beautiful statement of closure, ever enough. I do seriously doubt it...

Speeches and posturing in the name of such sadness seems to always fall woefully short. Death comes for everyone. It does not have to be planned and so deliberate. Be it one or 3000 or hundreds of thousands, death rings true of tragedy, especially when planned.

It could help to think, perhaps, that killing for any reason will someday be a past practice....

Unfortunately, it is still a thought. The killing will continue. The reality of Nine Eleven is that this was and is our house. Our families were at immediate risk, our mothers, fathers; children were being destroyed before our very eyes. Our very existence was being changed forever.

The thought of people leaping from towering buildings to their sure death rather than suffer a more horrible end is overwhelming just to think about. The ultimate collapse of the towers coming apart in fragments not unlike the worst child structure and then the fragments of human remains was unbearable for many and still is.

An endless search for these pieces of a person will never ever end. No, this day of death is different.

It has changed all our lives forever. So many things will never be or be like it was again.

The other dark days were "war" days, the casualties were the products of war. This was a sacred sacrifice by all that died and suffered through this horror. A sacrifice by mankind without any participant's or survivor permission.

These people were taken by hate and madness only to show how precious all life is and that the harmony of peace and acceptance of the brotherhood of mankind should demand all effort until realized...

Posted in Local, National, News, Politics, Social Interests, World | No Comments »

# Eavesdropping on the Junkie and the Wino

September 16th, 2011

An overheard conversation between two gentlemen of distinct choices went along these lines.

J: Did you feel the earthquake?

W: No, I don't think I did. I've been shakin' and quakein' for such a long time now I ain't too sure what I'm feelin'. Put some music on and I can make it look kinda cool.

J: "No man, come on be serious... but... I didn't feel it either. Just can't understand why people have to try to feel an earthquake... Did not have to ask about that one in Japan... huh? Nobody said too much about that lately either, right?"

W: "True that.... that "tsunami and water on the meltdown...whooooeee. Anything other than deal with some truth. Like they did to the Native Americans, Shoshone, Sioux, Apache or what tribe was unlucky that day. Just wanted to get on to somethin' else quick.... gave them some firewater though.

J: "Oh man, what in hell you talkin' bout?"

W: "Dealin' with the reality and some truth! They go way back with skippin' ova that.they make some boss firewater though.wish they slide me a taste or two.

J: "There you go again."

W: "Wasn't that a quote from a famous president?"

Posted in News, Parenting, Sports, Uncategorized | No Comments »

# The Presidency. Economy Stimulus 2011.

September 16th, 2011

The economy of this country has been rescued and revived from the larceny and mismanagement of the Bush administration.

The existing problems lie solely in the remnants of that pathetic group of obstructionists, liars, and selfish dimwits who happen to share the common ground of being separatists, elitists and racist to the core.

The initiatives by the present administration have resuscitated the auto industry, the financial support system and, provided the basis for a health care platform for all people. It has changed the foreign policy direction, diminished the cloud of terrorism and given a total plan for future progress. It has also done this without using "fear" as catalyst to intimidate the masses.

The presentation by the President for jobs was specific about the need and the cost. It was similar to the base used by FDR in his beginning as our leader. It was detailed in defining the goals and how they would be accomplished. It was detailed in why these goals were necessary to all Americans and how much it would cost and how it would be paid for.

The press didn't mention that it was so well received.

This was supposed to define the president's chances for reelection. Indeed, it reinforced that he was consistent and even more capable than expected.

That does not, however, guarantee his victory in 2012. He has completed and accomplished much in the face of obstacles and criticism without any recognition or collaboration or approval from the other "party "to this date. Amazing...

The press actually posted a "terrorist threat"thus far undocumented or active in any way immediately after his presentation. The presentation was obviously, hidden behind the false activity that followed to "protect our country" on this historically sad day. I contend that it was a farce purely to distract from the content that was in that "American Jobs" effort.

The Republicans are dedicated to denying reelection of this man. The inherent racism of my country lends ease to the distortion and the criticism. The social and economic separations are another obstacle that will diminish with jobs and equality in the application of our laws. The Republicans are totally against this and they have only exposed this weakness time and again.

The truth lies in the history of their inability to produce equality and justice for all Americans regardless of race, creed, or social status. They are totally incapable and this is a fact. What is worst is they are unwilling to make that commitment to fulfill the words of the founding fathers and make this a reality.

This fight is for all Americans if not mankind.

Posted in Health, Local, National, News, Politics, World | No Comments »

# Accountability, the time is now.

September 19th, 2011

This administration has settled and brought dignity and diplomacy to the chaos and illegal actions of the Bush administrations. The weaknesses that seemingly appear really lie only in the spines and knees of the Democratic Party that this President represents.

These Democrats are shallow in their commitment to the causes that were meaningful and brought change in 2008. The issues that then comprised substance to the people of this country seem to scare them now. The truths about the actions that made their election possible has shaken their ability to stand and be firm.

The crimes and breaches of behavior and government protocol perpetrated by the Republicans have appeared to intimidate them. They also harbor distrust of each other and share a lack faith in the ability to accomplish the goals and duties necessary to achieve them.

That said, accountability must be a mandate. For all concerned and for the continued growth of this nation, these things cannot go unaddressed.

A small capsule of these issues follows:

The Republican theft or misuse of treasury tax payer money:

Halliburton, and other so-called government sub-contractor's interests and duties need to be reviewed

The deeds of John Ashcroft and the people who were his allies are in that same basket

The lies to manipulate our involvement in war and the causing of American deaths in Iraq with the subsequent deaths of innocent citizens of that country.

The plunder of billions of American dollars from Iraq. Saddam's stash could finance the new budget.

The air would be so much easier to breathe if these "issues" were addressed and resolved to the eyes and ears of the public or the everyday citizen. We, the people, do care and want know. Knowing would provide a public example for us to be able to understand why we have been held to accountability for our misdeeds, regardless of our pain, anguish and embarrassment to our families.

This is justice and the foundation of the American way.Let the chips fall where they may. The time is now.

Posted in Local, National, News, Politics, World | No Comments »

# Life Support for the Republicans. Pathetic Democrats

September 19th, 2011

This is why the Republican Party still breathes.

Our Democratic party is nursing them constantly with their indecision and petty internal sniping.

This President is a really unique and persevering individual. His party needs to unify and be firm. Their lack of commitment to be supportive of him and their own colleagues in unity provides the strongest issue to be a pest. Unnecessarily.

There is not one Republican or any platform they seem to articulate worth the agony of repeating. If the Democrats were united now, they could accomplish the changes that they outline. This is a significant moment in America's history. This is a moment in which all the major issues in mankind's history can be focused on and directed to eventual resolution.

There is another, sad, but true fact.

Racism is so systemic, we all must be vigilant to be clear and focused. Yes, Obama's fellow Democrats are victims of this thinking. Blacks as well as whites suffer. The religious bigotry is equally sickening. The bias against independent thought and intelligence is another notable handicap.

This President is clearly intelligent, a necessary quality, I would think, in this position. Unfortunately, in politics and in this position, that has been lacking too often. Intelligence has triumphed throughout history. When coupled with courage it has made the cornerstones for mankind to build on.

An "intelligent approach" was on exhibit many times in this administration's efforts to fulfill the necessary demands of the crises in 2008. The latest and perhaps, a historical example, was the command

and coordination of the initiative needed to finally close the Osama Bin Laden issue. The piece-by-piece dismemberment of Al-Qaeda is a relief to the whole Middle East. The cabinet choices and their effective foreign policy is a reflection of their collective thinking collaboration.

His "American Jobs Act" is another piece in the quilt of this "thinking" progression.

The opposition, including some Democrats, in contrast, are not able to offer any platform of their own. None, except to project he won't be reelected in 2012.

It is sad, to me, that they allow this ilk some time or audience for their profiles.

Is this America at its best? No not yet, but the work is truly in progress. Intelligence and courage will triumph.

Posted in Health, Local, National, News, Parenting, Politics, World | No Comments »

# NFL Coach's Insider....

September 24th, 2011

Two of the best today were overheard on the QT...

A: "How ya doin?"

B: "So far so good, something like chinese food, ya know."

A: "Don't mention any food, man; you know it's my weakness."

B: "Not intentional to probe you like that. I was wonderin' what your schedule was looking like to you?"

A: "Hey got the Gezziants this week as Snoop would say. I love to play them since "Tom Terrific" has been coachin' them."

B: "Yes, that he is... he is one tight mf but he must be a nice guy or something' with all that luck to pull his cohones off the skillet, you know what I'm sayin?"

A: "I do, but he just seems to help me a lot. maybe 'cause I see his tight ass twice a year, at least. heh-heh."

B: "That David Tyree dookie won't happen again I bet you a fat man on that."

A: "You tryin' to be funny, Billy?"

B: "No. No. you just sensitive Andy. He just always has these hellacious players. That GM Jerry Reese really knows what is good. Every year he pulls some spectacular thug players out of the pile while everybody else is drawing blanks."

A: "Sheeeit, you got that right. If I had Tom "Predictables" players your ass would be grass I'd be John Deeree."

B: "If had his GM you and the rest of the league could kiss food good bye  oops, just messin' round man."

# The Giants. 2011

September 27th, 2011

Tom "Terrific" Coughlin was at his best yesterday. As a lifelong Giants fan; the win against the hated Philadelphia Eagles warmed my heart.

He, Tommy T, seemed to be forced to play the players he should have been playing all along. Actually, the coach's choices yesterday were right on the money.

Being a rabid fan, the Giant's losing will not be accepted by me. I was pretty good after this stalwart victory. It was a good feeling.

Tom, I am offering an apology for my criticism of you. One game, sometimes, is a lot. Evidently, you are a better coach than I thought. What is more important and apparent is that your players will play hard for you. That means everything when the chips are down. Congratulations.

A mere fan like myself, I am sure, would not know the intricacies of that job you have.

I do hope you remember the formula for your most stirring victory in a while. Victor Cruz, Brandon Jacobs, Ahmad Bradshaw with Eli Manning stirring the stew. These exceptional draftees and free agent picks of GM Jerry Reese again and again on offense and defense, and Special teams all together in this victory yesterday made a most satisfying remedy for the hunger that persisted since last season.

Posted in Social Interests, Sports | No Comments »

# Our lives at Risk....Capital Punishment

September 27th, 2011

The execution of Troy Davis was accomplished at 11:08 pm, 21 September 2011. He was convicted of killing a police officer over 20 years ago.

The world watched while a civilized nation sanctioned this act of barbarism.

Killing or murder is more popular than ever. I find that thought increasingly more discomforting. The fact that there is no effort or coordinated attempt that shows any progress to ending this madness is totally discomforting.

Killing is an accepted response to problems. The fact that these problems are never resolved by that dastardly final act seems to matter not. Any suggestion that can be offered to kill as a reason is listened to. All too often there is no reason at all offered. Actually, there is no reason that stands examination except self-defense in the most extreme and personal fashion.

The victims and the families of these crimes are just unfortunate additions to the casualty list.

It matters not what the "issue" or rational is or that may be stated. Killing by committee, as in crime punishment (court), war, endless religious bigotry and squabbles that have this "option," personal squabbles and discord only perpetuate more killing.

These organized and planned atrocities legitimatize and underwrite any sick individual's poor excuse for taking life in his own hands and in his own personal way and again, for any reason or non-reason.

Troy Davis became the latest in a long line of victims and "expendable" people. They will all be a cause forgotten in the near future. He will be replaced by the "latest" victim before I finish this sentence....

Posted in Health, Local, National, News, Politics, World | No Comments

# Eavesdropping on "The Wino and Junkie"

October 10th, 2011

W: My man, can I get some change?

J: Wish I could. Seems you always want change. Can't you go big? A dollar or "extra change"…?

W: "Hey, I got to go with what works. Not like those constipated republicans.can you believe those fools? Damn.they would be funny if they wasn't so stupid."

J: "Yes, yes, yes cannot believe this times.They so sorry they want to run a brother against another." "This shit done changed big time."

W: "Well you know they ain't that fast. heh heh." J: "That's that racial profile Man, don't go there."

W: "Hey, I ain't.this ain't physical.they not too quick with the feedback either.that bigot Texan tore hisself a new butthole…"

J: True dat, I think they throwin' in the towel so they can't say they lost to Bam.

W: "Yes, don't mess with Bam. Ask Al-Qaeda."

Posted in Local, National, News, Parenting, Politics, Social Interests | No Comments »

# The Truth about the Election of 2012 and the Republicans

October 10th, 2011

The election in 2012 will be a confirmation of 2008.

The press and the alarmists would offer otherwise but the facts cannot be argued or changed.

The Republican Party, as previously known, is finished.

There are those who would like to think that this is not true but, fortunately, it is. They, the Republicans, have endorsed this truth with their own personal actions and the group they have again chosen as leaders and candidates.

The Republican actions have been documented time and again in this column. At the risk of being redundant, I will repeat some of these truths again.

They are unabashed liars and prevaricators almost without exception. This party has run far off the sanity course with its attempts to continue the crimes of the past and plant seeds of separation and disharmony. The totally worthless and senseless actions that surface immediately are racism, social injustice and economic inequality.

Their crimes against humanity under the guise of war, economic budgeting" and the theft of money under the security of our "homeland" are sickening and truly add insult to injury.

They have stolen and manipulated the freedoms of our country and base principles. Truly unfortunate is their inability to change, accept change, or be honorable about accepting responsibility for their acts and intent, past or present. This is incriminating, if not damning.

The World is in constant change. The times, they too have changed. The ability to keep the truth unseen or unheard has passed. We all now have access to "information" without filter or distortion or false interpretation.

This is not the fifties or the sixties or the eighties, thankfully. We do now know and document, now ourselves freely. "There you go again" will not help any longer.

To say this again may seem a bit too much, but for those who do not yet read or understand, a strangely Republican consistency, here it is.

There is not one Republican candidate for the presidential election in 2012. Not one, yet. There will not be one from the pathetic group of misfits offered thus far. A contestant is a real stretch.

The reason is that they are simply unwilling or incapable of being honest to or caring about the American people.

All of us, the citizens of America, count. To be a margin more specific, all of the people of the world.count! We always did.

The actions of their most recent administration were forever criminal. Most egregious was their dishonesty and antisocial intentions for all mankind. They were an embarrassing moment without the option to apologize. They fostered a sad and truly tragic period in our history. They have offered nothing positive, nothing since to our American people.

These facts will surely eliminate the "contest" in 2012....

Posted in Local, National, News, Parenting, Politics | No Comments »

# Wall Street. The Movement for the masses

November 28th, 2011

A long time coming...

But the beginning has happened. The match has been struck and the flame is increasing and spreading. Two months ago, Occupy Wall Street began and has spread to cities and campuses around the country and world.

Here in the "wealthiest" nation on the planet a "movement" by the working class, now, joining hands with the unions and middle class out of work. History has offered a preview of these times. At the risk of scaring someone we will try to avoid those well-known "phrases."

The "working class" is a larger and more diverse group than defined as such in the past. The common factor with the past is still the difference in pay or income compared to the upper or "safe middle class" or the wealthy.

The 99% is now insisting on recognition, inclusion, the cessation of bigotry and a balance in the distribution of wealth.

The linkage around the globe, the changes in the governments in Libya, Egypt and Mid-East all ring with the sound of "change." This new world is connected and no filters or barriers can keep the truth from being known. This is a truly historic moment we are living in now.

The efforts thus far expended seem to have been slowed or measured and controlled. The desperate symptoms of revolution and upheaval have not yet taken place here or in many modern societies. There is a possibility that these drastic and often bloody moments may not be necessary for the eventual complete change.

The realities of today are channeled by overwhelming new technology and the fact that people are embracing education on every level. Literacy is now a shared blessing that fortifies the exchange of information and planning of events.

The qualities and vulnerabilities that we humans share far outweigh our petite trivial differences. The earth can provide for all of us in abundance providing we are caring and protective of each other. We have entered these times of change more united and with greater compassion than ever before. Wall Street is a fitting restart.

The movement shall not be any longer delayed.

Posted in Health, Local, National, News, Politics, Social Interests, World | No Comments »

# Eavesdropping on the Wino and Junkie....

November 28th, 2011

J: "How u livin' today?"

W: "Not as bad as yesterday, my mellow friend. Ate too much, family was wonderful 'til they got to fightin' over leftovers. I just got my jug and eased up out of there."

J: "Speaking of yesterday, the fresh air compared to the stench of that past administration is remarkable. People shoppin' travelin', laughin', goin' to school and everything. I didn't even get to my connection today.yet. and I am feeling pretty good."

W: "Yes, I even have another bottle in the stash didn't even drink it all. Can hardly believe getting a few greedy, selfish ass people out of the way can make such a difference."

J: "Got my 2012 t-shirt on discount too, Heh-heh. even got you one."

W: "Thanks, good looking out for me  seems people are doing more of that too."

J: "More of what?"

W: "Looking out for each other!"

J: "Oh right. I thought you were talking about making babies.  that's always a good thing to be doin'."

W: "Damn, there you go again."

Posted in News, Politics, Social Interests, World | No Comments »

# My Giants... at Peril

November 28th, 2011

The Coach Tom Coughlin is true to form.

A nice, probably, grandfatherly type guy without any imagination or ability to accept responsibility for failure. He has injured more players. He has insulted and put his best player's careers at risk. The fact that he has lost a game to any team is irrelevant.

The man is demoralizing his players and their fans and is injuring them with his self-destructive offense. He is totally incompetent. His inability to be fair or honest to himself or his players, especially Brandon Jacobs borders on criminal.

This coach is conducting a serial train wreck with his players, fans, GM and franchise as victims. He and he alone will be responsible for the health and career collapse of Eli Manning. He should be discharged ASAP or immediately...

The owners, Mara and Tisch should be ashamed of themselves for keeping him if not for ever hiring him.

The Giants have managed to represent a professional positive as a team because they have the best players on one team in the league.

Jerry Reese, the GM, is a genius. Through draft picks and free agency, he and he alone manage the payroll and replace the players with the "best athlete "every year. He does not deserve to have his Giant career fixed to Tom Coughlin. Eli Manning is the best quarterback in the league. His career deserves new coaching and leadership from that level.

Receiving corps, linebackers, defense line, corner backs, Jerry Reese gets "players." Draftees, that start, and free agents that are the cream at their position, he gets them and signs them without fanfare and within the budget.

This is a unique brilliant gift for my beloved Giants and should no longer be wasted and misused. A new coaching staff is mandatory and is much easier to acquire than gifted athletes. in the prime of their lives.

Posted in National, News, Social Interests, Sports | No Comments »

# The Election of 2012. Democracy, a Work in Progress

December 20th, 2011

In 2008 Barack Obama was elected president of the United States. His opponents were John McCain and Sarah Palin. They represented the Republican Party at that time after a tedious and embarrassing search through assorted misfits, liars and political criminals.

The Bush administration, Republican, which had been in office for eight years, was a gross disaster of epic proportions. Killing thousands of people in wars that were fostered on the American table by lying to the congress and the people of the United States, they pressed on.

They destroyed the economy, the financial stability, national industries (Banks, Auto) and then plundered the resources while sending the national debt to depths that seemed unrecoverable. They left office slinking away. Totally unable to be public in support of their new candidates or show their presence, these greedy racists remain in the shadows.

It remains a burning curiosity of mine that they can still continue their lives without being held accountable. They and they alone caused the deaths of over four thousand American armed forces personnel and an estimated one million innocent Iraq citizens.

Their depravity has resulted in the destruction and end of the Republican Party as we once knew it. The remnants of that sordid group cannot show their public presence in support of any one or group without bringing the stigma of stench with them.

I, for one, will not mourn their demise or the death of that party. The thinking that prevailed is still being nurtured and fed. We, the people, are left with a pitiful choice from the usual suspects who cannot stomach themselves on the morning after exposure. Their friends, families and the nation wince in reflection. The agony remains from their long period of greed, racist and separatist design.

The Republicans did not own these flaws alone. These are human faults at large, unfortunately. The Republicans did employ and reinforce these human cruelties with emphasis and without any intention to change or be humane in this last Bush administration.

It has taken a sharp contrast in executive leadership to show how these dastardly political maneuvers affect everyone clearly.

These activities and the thinking that propels them have no place in a democratic society. These manipulations cannot be clothed or hidden ever again. The people that employ those ills are no longer acceptable in any way especially on the ballot.

However, within a Democracy, a work in progress must continue to persist. The dredges of society that previously prevailed still exist. The examples lie in people like Gingrich, Bachmann, Tea party affiliates that threaten constantly to disrupt any progress.

Having managed to promote some sadistic, selfish, mentally petite individuals into Congress, they have managed to hinder all movement for the good and welfare of all Americans and humans at large. These dingleberries will do anything to obstruct the passing of laws that would make life worth living for the minority and for the majority.

They cannot reverse the passing of a health act that has the possibility of insuring care for everyone. They cannot alter the fact that unemployment is ending... I repeat, ending, in a rush. They cannot continue making war and killing innocent armed forces personnel and humans of other countries like they did in Iraq. They cannot terrorize our population and future with pretending to search for a creep like BinLadin and his Al-Qaeda cronies while stealing from the taxpayer with bankrupting bills from their chosen corrupt suppliers. The soldiers are home from Iraq.

They still stubbornly and with unbelievable stupidity choose to use any ploy to obstruct this administration. The reason is simple. They are racists and separatists, children of the same and reared amongst the lies and inhumanity of that thinking. They cannot accept the fact that it was all a huge lie. A horrendous crime against all humanity and the slave was not the only victim. A crime that my country, America, has to eventually cleanse from its very soul and in the process, perhaps, from the planet.

No, that time is thankfully over and the removal of its remains are being swept from Iraq and the mid-east methodically. It is being weeded out of our government with a patience and respect that can only come in a Democracy, governed with thought and purpose and supported by a people committed to freedom and justice for all.

This "Democracy"...is taking hold after that stunning result of 2008.

Posted in Local, National, News, Politics, Social Interests, World | No Comments »

# Another Year in Our Lives....

January 20th, 2012

Many things happen daily in our lives. Some of these things are planned and some are not. We accept and deal with these things or events and continue on as a part of our "living" process. In this process we have the option of choice and the choices we make often dictate the events that follow.

Not wanting to be personal but the choices we make in our government often dictate our quality of life. On a long-term basis, yearly, or for decades, these choices affect our daily life as we try to fit our other choices around them. They, those "choices" could very well expand into life-or-death moments.

Therein lies our prognosis for our future and the future of our family and our larger family, humanity.

It seems to me that in earlier moments of time we were limited by our lack of ability to communicate freely and by our lack of ability to understand information due to educational short comings and fear that was not softened by religious dogma or leaders that were selfish and inhumane.

All of these conditions have changed as we progressed in time and some conditions have disappeared. We can now communicate through technology freely and without an "interpreter." We are much more collectively "literate" and education is being valued and appreciated all over our planet we now understand what we want to, on our terms and our own personal values.

This sets the table for 2012 and all that we may choose to address in this year. One of the events scheduled for this year and every four years forward is the election of our leaders here in the United States of America.

Ours is a relatively new nation by comparison, and collectively is a composite of all the nations and cultures of this planet. Our country is unique in that fashion and simultaneously contains all the differences that constitute the fragments of human life everywhere. I am so proud that I am an American, if I had to be nationalistic. One of my earlier Chess buddies called me a "cosmopolite." I liked that too even though I am still not sure just what he meant.

The structure of all governments, rise or fall on the people. In this new nation, America, we have rapidly passed through many stages of human social change and even reform. The election of 2008 presented many options but only two clear choices. These choices were to go on as in the past or to embrace the truth and honesty of the reality we were confronted with. My country chose the latter.

Part of the past was the human resource that is reflected in The Republican party. This group of individuals managed to compile all of the sick and most detrimental traits of humanity in their actions and purpose into the last or Bush administration.

They not only exhibited these revolting habits at large but they reveled in them. They compounded the felonies over and again with lies and hypocrisy. They made my nation see that those past habits were not to be tolerated or continued. They brought about the need for change and brought change into a necessary reality.

Now, let me be first to say we are all faulty, being human. We all possess some if not all of the weaknesses that these Republicans show. However, I, for one, want to be a "better" person as I live. I want others to be treated honestly and fairly. I want to live and live well but not at the expense of others. I, above all, want the freedom and equality and justice for all of my human family. I realize that this may not happen in my life time. It may very well be a work in progress as long as we humans have life. This progress must continue as I see and feel it. I am sure now more than ever that it will.

Going back to the past, the racism, elitism, bigotry at all levels, murder, and general disregard for "other" humans is finished, over, history. We, as a people, represented at large here in the United States, have implemented change. We are in progress now.

The Republican Party as we knew it has not accepted that fact. The sordid group of people that are offered as representatives are clear reflections of their lack of honesty, with themselves to say nothing of others. They are an abominable group. It is sad that because of their commitment to being racist, clearly, above all other faults, they would rather wallow in their porcine feces rather than embrace the beginning of a new time for all humanity.

Posted in Local, National, News, Politics, Social Interests, World | No Comments »

# The Last Gasp of the Republican Party

January 29th, 2012

This month has given the world the benefit of witnessing an important phase of the American democracy at work. What a benefit it is. The Republican caucus and other primaries produced three different winners. Yes, I did say "winners." Winners that left the country whining and moaning. Having said time and again, in every way possible how deplorable this group is, it never ceases to amaze me how completely lax or slow the media is about being honest to the public. I will not put much effort into clearing the media's faults. Some of them I am sure are part of a greater or lesser plan that I am not aware of as a whole.

I will attempt to remind those that need reminding that this "group" is the same ilk that were feverishly active in the past administration's actions. The last winner had the gall to proclaim and that he was the best choice because he was the only candidate that could unseat the incumbent or plainly put "get the black man out of the White House."

Yes, that's what I said. This so-called candidate offers that premise as his only value.

So that is their goal? The goal of the Republican Party is to get "him" out of the white house.

Foreign policy, well-being of citizens, education, erasing terrorism all is secondary. The curious attempt at criticizing the economy rings true of serious mental deficiencies at every level.

Briefly, claiming a "slow rate of recovery and high unemployment "is an insult to our intelligence. The ability to continue these insults appears to be the Republican commitment more and more, especially when looking at their acts and inability to remember the past and how this prevailing crisis was developed.

They have exhibited a total lack of cooperation for any effort from this administration at every level particularly in addressing the recovery effort. The economy was on the verge of the second "Great Depression" (the first in '33 was under a Republican administration also) when one of their groups stated as early 2009 that their objective was making certain Obama would not be reelected.

They have used any and every political maneuver to obstruct, delay or defeat any Democratic initiative. In spite of their efforts to "impede" for lack of a better word, we are seeing 20 consecutive months of private sector job growth without their help in any way.

The last gasp offers a clueless millionaire who steals and takes jobs from the poor, a nice conservative naiveté who clearly needs mothering desperately, a elderly citizen who is not taking all his meds and last but not least, a decadent egotistical liar, without grace, self-respect, any memory or morals by his own admission.

Can we mercifully remove life support?

# The Deliverance of the Giants. or the Genius of Jerry Reese

January 29th, 2012

It seems that I and the Giant world must continue to live with Coach Tom Coughlin. On the eve of preparation for a return to the Super Bowl with the formidable New England Patriots, the success of winning the last five games in a row would make it a difficult time to change coaches.

The question surely is fitting as to why a change would be necessary after such success. A moot question at best because he will be staying. The answer never the less is forthcoming.

He, Tom Coughlin, chooses a very strange and dangerous method of utilizing his players. He gives no recognition to his players unless urged. He has caused players to be hurt and waived due to personal issues. The misuse of Brandon Jacobs, for one, the over exposure of the great Eli Manning to injury for the other.

On Brandon Jacobs, he has chosen to NOT give this great player consistent opportunities to run the ball. Consistent being 20-25 carries per game. This a critical factor with big running backs and a religious factor in football by all other coaches with a powerful runner. The use of D.J. Ware and the abuse of Ahmad Bradshaw, with a critical injury to his foot are the options he has chosen this year. The cost is lack of ball control, excessive exposure of defense and losses to Seattle and Washington etc. It is no accident they have to make their run on the Super Bowl on "the road" again, rather than the friendly home field in the Meadowlands. Brandon is a healthy 6'4? running back who can catch, block and run the forty-yard test in 4.5 seconds or better.

On Eli Manning over exposure to possible injury due to predictable passing attack and unnecessary physical pounding by opponent's defense.What are the Giants without Eli?

This is a personal opinion obviously, and I have attempted to express these errors in prior Giant posts.

The larger problem is that his strategies make winning more difficult and an uncertainty until the game is over. He is blessed with the best GM in the NFL and never ever gives recognition or credit in any way to this GM or the plethora of excellent players he is provided with.

Players have a limited time to be at their best in athletics. The possibility of injury and other interruptions to careers are a reality of life. Winning is the only goal and winning is what the Giants have managed to do recently to save his job. He has existed on the edge of being fired many times. It is a wonderful fact that the Giants have continued to win. They win in spite of Coach Coughlin's ill decisions and mismanagement.

The Giants win because of superior personnel, players to be more specific. In this difficult time of limited payroll flexibility and free agency the Giants are stocked with outstanding football players at every position it seems. Eli is the elite and resourceful leader that quarterbacks must be. Running backs, linemen on offense and defense, special teams, wide receivers, it goes on and on. No other team in the NFL has these stalwart athletic people at every position.

This is because the Giants General Manager is a genius. He knows football and he knows who can play the game and who cannot. He knows the business end and how to negotiate with the agent representatives of the players. His name is Jerry Reese.

He did not choose this coach. I am certain he would be open to selecting another if the opportunity or need was there. He is proven truly uniquely competent because the players he selects cannot lose for long. They are simply too good.

Football is played on the field by the players. That fine edge of being a consistent and dominant winner comes with the knowledge of what to use and when to use it. Coaching is the element that makes the difference here.

Coughlin will win because of his players. He will also cost the Giants great opportunity to be immortal by injuring players and letting them be waived for other teams to benefit. He will cost the Giants home field advantage by losing games to weaker teams in the season. He will kill the opportunity for immortality by misusing the athlete or worse not using him at all. Jerry Reese cannot remedy this. Ownership has given Coughlin an "extended" stay over and again. I do wonder if he would be getting these chances if he was minority member.... But that is a subject for another day.

I am a loyal Giant fan.

I, too, am ecstatic when they win. I am certainly glad Coach Coughlin can smile. Winning must be a great laxative too.

Posted in Local, National, News, Social Interests, Sports | No Comments »

# Duty Driver Day

February 27th, 2012

This day began approximately eleven months after June 6, 1960. Private Tan Renrut entered the U.S. Army on that day. I suppose if he had wanted to, he could have checked the date those southern Americans burned at interstate commercial bus down to the wheels. Then he would know what day he had been assigned to duty driver.

Tan chose to enter the armed forces after spending his first year in college. He was a student in good standing at Wayne St. University. Never failed a course was what he told me. He needed insurance for the baby his college girlfriend was beginning to swell with, so he joined the Army hoping for a career after Officer Candidate School and a glorious experience as warrior in his country's service.

Of course, he could have chosen to not marry her or even to abandon her but Tan had a conscience and this wasn't the first pregnancy in his life. Surely this child would have been aborted or something else, he thought, if he didn't "do the right thing." He had felt the pain and shame of abortion from his high school sweetheart's tragedy and he was humbled and traumatized by that. To think of what she had endured was forever a sharp pain in his psyche and soul.

He and his college buddy were really close. They spent all available time together and making love continuously, effortlessly, intensely... playing singing and dancing. Yes, that was what they did... Young love it was... So, he married this African American with pretty blue eyes... Yes, from Louisiana with blue eyes, a really fine-looking thing she was. What a body too... She was also smart and self-respecting in every way but she was pregnant. They married and he went to Ft. Knox, Kentucky. They were eighteen years old.

She went to live in New Jersey with his family while he pursued his career in the Army. Basic training followed in Ft. Benning, Ga. With advanced individual training at Ft. McClellan Ala.

A moment here to reflect on Tan's upbringing. It was in the northeast US. His neighborhood was ethnically and culturally mixed but it did seem odd that often whites hung with whites and blacks/negroes stayed with their own. It was unwritten in the Northeast... just... seemingly "understood." Tan had difficulty understanding that. He chose his friends and foes freely on both sides of the fence. He lived on the border street of the white school district. Not knowing that was why he had been attending the "white" schools. He was comfortable wherever he sat.

The white policemen were nasty he thought but they had a nasty job. He thought it went with the territory. His families were proud African-Americans. They took serious pride in being black and being proud of the heroes of that day. Joe Louis, Jackie Robinson, Sugar Ray Robinson, Kid Gavilan, Nat King Cole, Ella Fitzgerald, Sarah Vaughn, Billy Eckstine. Oh, hell yeah... they all were so damn good, his Dad always said. His Dad was a great baseball player would have been in the majors if they hadn't been segregated. Everybody in his family was "good-lookin" and could dance and sing all they wanted to. His family thought that the one or two black policemen were Toms but they did have a job so that wasn't the worst thing. They were not friends of the family though and definitely didn't deserve to be trusted.

Tan didn't realize the Army was "integrated" only eight years before his induction. He had only been in the south twice on his Uncle John's farm briefly when he was four years old. His grandfather was a WWI vet and father WWII vet. He was made to be a soldier.

He left Ft. Knox due to crowding and was convoyed by the Army to Ft, Benning, Ga. Encountering racism all the way, he was baffled. "It did not make sense to me," he told me.

Signs at gas stations and restaurants said "We Don't serve no niggers" water coolers with "white only" on them while rusty pipes with water running out were signed "for colored."

This was 1960 United States of America, his country, he knew. He did not know this. "It really was pissing me off," Tan said but "I kept my cool."

Eleven months later he had been assigned to Ft. McClellan after Chemical Corps School. He had been waiting to be processed to OCS for five months. Naive, but no longer blind, Tan did his duty. McClellan was also the Basic Training post for the Women's Army Corps. So, with Chemical, Biological and Radiological warfare as his MOS he had the liberty of sharing a post where the women outnumbered the men six to one. He did not ever think that his Officer School papers were being trashed. That his prolonged stay there was deliberate because of the racism that is still systemic in his country. No Tan was too naive to go there... then.

Then that Sunday in May came. Tan was assigned to be Post duty driver. Not the worst duty he thought. Class "A" uniform,... his style... loved his spit shined boots... five creases starched shirt/Khakis. It was a warm sunny spring day, slow.Everything seemed to be on easy that day.

The First Lieutenant, officer of the day, summoned Private Tan Renrut to his office. Told him he was to go into town to pick up a Colonel coming in from Ft. Belvoir, Va. at the bus station. The town, 13 miles south of the fort, was Anniston, Ala.

Private Renrut was driving a U.S. Army loden green sedan, four door, 1960 Chevrolet with official white numbers and lettering. A stick shift on the column, Private Renrut was in his element driving. The bus from Belvoir/ Washington was due in at 1700 hrs. It was 1630 hrs. when he pulled his official vehicle up in front of the Anniston Bus Depot.

There was a mob, major mob, in front, men and women, mostly men in front. They were blocking the driveway which exited in the front and the buses entered in a circular fashion from the rear. Private Renrut exited his vehicle and started for the driveway but the mob cursing and uttering racial slurs and epithets were blocking his way. He knew them by now. Armed with farm tools, old rifles, shotguns, sticks, axes, teeth missing they were a sorry lot he thought. Fear wasn't there at all then. Just some crazy ass crackers on the shuffle were the way he processed it. He walked around the mob and up the driveway to the "colored" entrance.

Something was strange though. He could feel it in the air. He walked proud and strongly into the station. He saw the porter as he heard him exclaim. "God Damn, Boy" Wat you doin' in here." He was on his knees scrubbing the floor. Renrut was startled. "I came to pick up a Colonel coming in on the bus from Washington" he said to the porter. The porter's face was twisted with fear. His eyes were bulging as he said "You better get yo ass outa here. Them damn peckerwoods done burn the bus down to wheels and riotin" and beatin peoples all up all over the damn place..."

"Then my heart was beating" Renrut told me.Beating so fast and hard I could feel it like a drum on the outside of me.He jumped in the phone booth and called the fort. The lieutenant answered and Tan told him the news.The Lieutenant said "Oh Shit, I forgot about that Renrut, forget about the Colonel and come back to the fort."... and hung up. Tan didn't have to call him back for instructions or help.He knew he was on his own...

Before he exited the colored depot, he knew that his vehicle was parked in the front with that mob of crackers around it and all in the driveway but he was thinking, using those innate instincts from his deepest kidnapped ancestors. I am walking out towards the back was his plan, walking until I get around the curve and then I am going to run like hell around to the front they will be following me but I will be... running like hell by the time they get to the top.

As he walked out the door and headed to the back, he heard someone say "there's one maybe he wants some too." He was on total edge now but he stayed with the calm walk until he turned the curved corner of the upper driveway then he busted it out combat boots, class "A" uniform on the double time like never before... They were running behind him. He saw his vehicle and was getting his keys out as he came up on it. Opening the door, key in ignition, starting it up all in the same moment the women had remained by the car. One jumped on the hood as the car kicked over. He was putting pedal to the metal as he shifted and popped that clutch. Took that biddy for a short ride on the hood before she fell off to the side....

Now, he was moving through Anniston and he was thinking too. With tears in his eyes, about being in uniform ready to give his life for his country, their country, about his father and all the others who had gone before him, worked and died. For THIS?. To be chased and.... he seethed....

He was going to be sent to Germany rather than be processed to OCS from here he had been told. His grandmother had sent his wife and six week old son to be with him in "Bama that past Christmas because "married people should be with each other if they could."

He thought and seethed some more. He was going to have to take the bus with them on it to wherever to get out of Anniston.

He stopped at the Black Cab station and bought his first pistol for $12.00...

No, they were not going to do this to him or his family.... He had it on him at the ready as he and his small family boarded the bus to Atlanta two weeks later....

A true story....

Posted in Local, National, News, Politics, Social Interests, World | No Comments »

# Unfinished Business-Election of 2012

May 30th, 2012

Memorial Day is still the 30th of May. The parades were a thrill to me as a youth. My country at war for the defense of freedom, ours and the "free" world, was always a theme to remember.

The caissons, warplanes, artillery and weapons of war exhibited in the parades were tools and symbols of what remained from the fallen brave and valiant men and women that died for this country. The many portraits of cemeteries with their endless ranks and files of crosses were reminders that freedom came at a price. A staggering price that often was coupled with horrific details of the battles and the slaughter as part of a great plan for victory to preserve our freedoms and ultimately, our American way of life.

These freedoms have been echoed many times. Freedom of speech and the freedom to choose our leaders or representatives come to my mind now.

The freedom to vote to choose our elected leaders is monumental and paramount. For many Americans it was not available. Many methods were employed to deny this freedom. The disenfranchised were minorities, women, and the economically challenged. That era is coming to a rapid end, bit by bit, election by election. My country, the United States of America, is the leader of nations embracing and enforcing the right to these freedoms.

The last four years have passed with unusual speed and intensity. I am of the opinion both factors were rooted in the fact that the United States of America was being led by a man committed to keeping his promises and capable of independent thinking while governing and getting "things" done with courage, intelligence, grace and integrity.

The Presidency itself is a seat birthed in pressure by definition. The occupant, Barack Obama, an African American, made every move, every word, every decision a subject of scrutiny, controversy and immediate critique because he is the first non-white to hold this office.

A man of extraordinary energy and charisma, President Obama brought sanity and a feeling of "understanding" foreign relations to the common man. His administration has ended a criminal war in Iraq while rescuing the auto industry and financial institutions. He has pulled the economy out of free fall and certain depression.

Now we stand on the edge of the election 2012....

My glaring disappointment in this President is for not "cleaning house." The Republican administration, G.W. Bush/Cheney, etc. were totally criminal in many ways in their last opportunity. That administration lied to congress and the American people. That administration killed over one million Iraq citizens with lies and manipulations. They raped and pillaged one of the most ancient and culturally rich nations of this planet. They sat while terrorists planned the deaths of thousands of Americans. They employed thieves of the Defense budget like Halliburton and other "private" profiteers. That administration was directly responsible for the deaths and casualties of over a hundred thousand American armed forces personnel. Governing with fear as an alternative threat at every turn, they wrecked home security and travel freedom forever by not pursuing the terrorist leads and condoning the al-Qaida gang. Which, was simply that, a "gang" with impotent leadership, that is being erased by President Obama's military and security leadership.

These Republicans fostered racism to the maximum. Fueled by greed, elitism, and absolutely evil intent they robbed the surplus. They slept on the national threat warnings and sent the economy into a free fall, a depression with their larcenous financial plots. They promoted doomed institution policies and a heartless approach to labor that wrecked the auto industry. They continuously threatened unions with other maneuvers. This is, in fact, what the President inherited when he won the election of 2008. Equality mandates equal justice for all.

Why weren't they prosecuted? Yes, the spineless self-serving Democrats who supported these policies should be included.

This lapse has set the table for the Tea party. It has given exposure to a sordid primary process of opponent dribble with the Republican opponent, after a putrid selection of choices, finally, a clueless veteran of elite mental vacuums and detachment from reality with not one shred of integrity or ability for beginnings. This "postponement" has allowed time to have some discussion for his and their "sick" perspectives.

Bottom line or to be blunt, this election is about Racism at the core and self-impressed controlling elitists desperately trying to continue their decadent inhuman practices into the future.

Healthcare, Education and Civil Rights, specifically Gay's right to marriage are issues that are being reset presently to the benefit of mankind and not just the United States alone.

Sadly, this has promoted conversations that contained speculation on how can the Republican Party is ever again taken seriously.

Their refusal to be honest or humane is overwhelming. It has been offered that these Republicans are the dimwitted descendants of the founding fathers from Europe's trash pile. Some distinguished "founding Fathers" were "evicted" from Europe. Their religion and their daily practices were deemed less than sensible or even tolerable as far back as the 17th century. Yes, they were told to leave the continent or face the gallows. Our luck has some them as our forefathers.

The Native American was the first casualty of these charming immigrants. That this group has been mating for four hundred years with the descendants of the pile of trash that was in Oglethorpe's Georgia colony leads to a really scary horror movie plot except this is not the movies.

In my loose imaginings, no other option seems to lead toward such evil and stubborn resistance to progress.

As a proud American on this Memorial Day, I eagerly look forward to the freedom for the right to vote... Again.

This time for confirmation of the progress we have started. This time with the hope that the unfinished business will be addressed to honor all that has been sacrificed and died for. This time to eliminate the current possibilities of threats to our peace, our liberty, and our individual pursuit of happiness forever.

Posted in Local, National, News, Politics, Social Interests, World | No Comments »

# The Last Gasp of the Republican Party Flatline

August 21st, 2012

A candidate who cannot bare himself or his taxes or defend his actions at this time in an election year?

A candidate who has chosen as his running mate a total neophyte bigot in an election year?

A Presidential candidate who will possibly be in deep inquiry just in time for election day   for a series of unsavory civil/criminal

activity? (taxes again)....

A party that has clearly confirmed a lack of respect for the tenets of a moral humane society by their actions and past and present.

Sounds terminal to me....

Let us review the list of social diseases that have bought this pathetic party to the edge of its final resting place:

Racism

Dishonesty

Greed

Disrespect and subjugation of our Mothers, Daughters, Sisters.... WOMEN?

Short list? These are so systemic in their character anything more is way too much for this epitaph.

These attributes are human and surely the Democrats have their share of kindred vermin. It seems curiously significant that at this time in human history that our beloved Republican party represents the core of these maladies and are willing to die with these convictions.

To accept accountability for their injustices and accept the growth in mankind and mankind's ability to know more truth now is beyond their conscience.

This last congress is a vivid example of their self-serving nature. Unfortunately, it, this very "nature," is rooted in the darker, no pun intended side of history. Their need to obstruct all ventures from the executive branch and to challenge existing law purely for the retardation of progress is damning. They refuse to govern for the good of the nation?

To resist change and persist at the pursuit of their personal goals with such stubborn determination while avoiding accountability for their deeds and commitments, at the risk, of all the sacred virtues of government, is unforgivable. Their despicable habits have joined to form the internal cannibalism that consumes them.

I, for one, will not mourn these people. I will not mourn the end of the elitists, the end of the bigotry they all have in common. I will not mourn the end of the lies throughout their history and the mistreatment of the common man.

While witnessing the growth of Democracy in this unique nation through human struggle with all the pain and anguish is satisfying, the best reward is knowing the past is truly behind us.

We must demand accountability for the Bush/Cheney administration's lies and criminal actions. Justice is mandate in an equal society.

We must no longer accept the inequality applied to women.

We must no longer tolerate partisan representation of the Congressional self-serving buffoons who seek to perpetuate the ills of the past cloaked in their petty diversion and divisive agendas.

I sincerely look forward to the future lined with the promise of better times…. a better community…. a better America. and world.

Posted in Local, National, News, Politics, Social Interests, World | No Comments »

# Our Lives at Risk....

August 24th, 2012

A movie theater in Colorado and a place of worship in Wisconsin. A jogger on a path in Pennsylvania and a series of similar sequels on Long Island. Minorities in their neighborhoods, homes and in transit is where we are dying.

Does the impact of lost of life diminish when there are more than one that dies in that tragic unnecessary moment? How about every life being in peril as long as the present approach remains in place. Everyone... including you and me, our family, our friends. at constant risk unless we, the living, take immediate action to stop the killing.

Easier said than done is too casual and careless a statement to be the final stop in this case.

I, for one, do treasure living this life and I would like to think that everyone alive would want to continue living. Limited exceptions to this personal declaration excluded, I am contending that an immediate plan to stop the killing is imperative.

If people are committed to continue killing regardless of our actions, then our directives could begin with enforced methods to control or limit the tools of death. A positive place to begin is the insistence of STRIDENT GUN CONTROL laws. When strictly enforced this effort will show the beginnings of success immediately by the decrease in deaths.

We must start some place and although that seems to be a monumental challenge, I am sure the plan to build the Pyramids was also. It was done!

While borrowing many things from Egyptian culture this practice lends me to believe that following the brick by brick (pyramid) approach would eventually make this a done deal.

Okay, a long time before completion is a given. The Pyramids building project was a long time work in progress too.

We must, nevertheless, immediately begin. NOW.... this act and other similar efforts....

Before we will be guilty of being accessories to murder, or victims!

Posted in Local, National, News, Parenting, Politics, Social Interests, World | No Comments »

# The Election of 2012. in a nutshell

September 8th, 2012


The last forty-six months has been a period of constant turmoil within the elective process. The ability to get any production out of congress and the leaders of any state that did not vote for Obama was nonexistent.

This 2012 election is fueled by the inherent systemic racism that still plagues our country. Although it has been a declining influence on the planet as a whole, Racism is perhaps the oldest of the demons that wreaks havoc on mankind. There are others not to be addressed here and now because of the urgency in dealing with this one that is the fuel and the engine for this election.

This chameleon devil, Racism, has managed to be decried only by victims and only when the current tragedies had managed to lose the disguise of a secondary opinion as a cause.

The election of a non-white leader to the head of the free world has ignited a political bedlam in the U.S. His success in spite of constant obstruction by the rival party has brought this coming election to significance unequaled in our history. All holds have been lifted. The false sense of acceptance and peaceful cohabitation has been under intense scrutiny and constant reflection. The feeling in some hearts cannot be hidden or individually suppressed any longer. The lies and sordid attempts to disrupt and eliminate the freedoms of the founding fathers have been endless.

The Republican Convention in Tampa at this time speaks volumes about this factor being the staple. The attendees are sadly, bigots with no plan to lead our nation or to set examples for anything except the lowest and most inhuman practices possible in a democracy. The themes on economics and unemployment are valid issues but the problem since 2008 has been the skin color of the current President.

Since that very day these assorted bigots have done nothing but cringe and recoil at the reality of having lost the election to a minority member of darker complexion. Three years and more of silly vicious efforts to obstruct any progress of any kind in the Congress without compassion for any other cause or effort was and is their mantra.

Their propaganda has made Joseph Goebbel's lies for Nazi Germany seem almost infantile in scope and productive cost.

The People of this party are throwing nuts at news media of nonwhite skin. The callous disrespect for women rights has been confirmed as party platform.

To continue to lie and to distort all truths just to enhance their elective possibilities is expected but the fact that this has been in the hearts of so many Americans all their lives is astonishing and a shame.

Fortunately for everyone, their sick efforts have only exposed the lack of character and values of this terminal party.

Only a true democracy can provide such wonderful contrast and opportunity to choose without an overwhelming human sacrifice in flesh and blood.

Posted in Health, Local, National, News, Parenting, Politics, World | No Comments »

# The New York Giants.... emergence of a repeat

September 8th, 2012

The best team in the NFL is the Giants. This team is deep and talented at every position. These exceptional athletes are being recruited and signed by the best GM in the NFL, Jerry Reese.

The off season has seen the usual transition but in this process the Giants have become ever stronger. The only vulnerability is in the coaching. Mr. Reese has supplied the coaches with such consistent and effective players they will win in spite of Tom Coughlin as they did in 2011.

To mention their names would only provide a list. Eli Manning is close to irreplaceable. His alternate is as good as alternates get. Yet we certainly do not want Eli hurt. Coach Coughlin exposes him and others to unnecessary risk. His defensive line will surely be a part of future folklore, assuming they are not depleted by being placed in negative positions by the failure of Tom's poor use of offense opportunities.

The necessary exposure to injury in football is a constant with every team but for the Giants they must endure the ill decisions of Coach Coughlin. He and he alone is responsible for risking the health of Eli and others due to his curious decisions.

I am as always, a total Giant fan so I, too, must accept the Coach's ill use of running backs and receivers. I am without a doubt thankful for GM Reese.

We will win this year... again. in spite of Coach Coughlin.

Posted in Health, Local, National, News, Social Interests, Sports | No Comments »

# Eavesdroppin on the Wino and Junkie Say what?

September 8th, 2012

W: My man.... is that you standing... up?

J: Very funny.... what a friend you are!

W: Don't tell me you are sensitive? Thinking? He he Damn! All wide-eyed and alert? Is something on your mind today?

J: Watching and listening to these political... "conventions". can be revealing if the media were...

W: They are necessary, the media is, and they are so plentiful.... all kinds all over the place.

J: Not where I was going... Do you have to interrupt all the time? If the media was more forthright and not often couching their words to allow meaningless distractions to prevail....

W: Uh—Oh. You are showing signs of paranoia or sumpin...

J: Now my faculties are 'slippin" because I tell it like it is.... sometime....

Anyway, when are they going to own what this election has been birthed in and nurtured? Racism! That is the whole issue... Nothing... else.

W: Okay... and? This is the U.S. and that is not news!

J: That's the point. Women's rights, Wars, Economy, Abortion, Health care all are addressed over and again. but being Black is not, at least, not on the front page... hmmmm... It is a double shame...

W: You are paranoid or sumpin... Bam is 50% and...

J: That is more than enough in the U.S.... Louisiana constitution

defines a person "Being Black" if said person has one black great- great grandparent....

W: Damn... you been booking up too?

J: Not really... The issue is about a black president being the leader

of this nation and thereby the free world. These damn bigots are turning in their graves.... ONLY THAT

W: Wow... You are right again... maybe... er left.... heh-heh...Pun?

J: Not funny....Will they, the media, ever get to defining how human or humane a candidate and their policies are?

Posted in Health, Local, National, News, Parenting, Politics, Social Interests, World | No Comments »

# The Debate... 2012 Election

October 9th, 2012

The election of 2012 is a monumental struggle in democracy. The elements and the factors combine to emphasize the importance of these results to be one of the most significant in history.

The incumbent, Barack Obama, was to say the least, as unimpressive as he was disappointing, even to his most loyal supporters.

There were many opportunities to expose the GOP candidate as an unabashed liar and opportunistic manipulator that were left unattacked. That omission posed many questions that should have been sealed in valid confirmation by facts before offered and confronted immediately when spoken by this hysterical maniacal mouth.

Truth was stretched constantly and my curiosity abounds as to why and how this behavior is permitted. It joins my endless questioning of the lack of prosecution for the crimes of the last GOP administration.

Being a mere citizen, a true member of the 47% that the GOP has no use for, I admit to being a bit clueless as to the approach of our President, and to what strategy will be employed in the next encounter.

It has been offered, in casual places, that there is a method to this madness. That method being in giving Mr. Romney an opportunity to expose his weapons/tools and his lack of respect for rules of order and social manners, our President does not have to bear criticism for being a "angry minority" or letting the truth flow freely without being interrupted.

It certainly makes the next debate more interesting and compelling.

Posted in Local, National, News, Parenting, Politics, Social Interests, World | No Comments »

# The Giants... A Dynasty in Progress

December 4th, 2012

The New York Giants are the best team in the National Football League. There is a problem with making that declaration at thiTs time because their record reflects another truth. It is not the best record. Their losses reveal a painful inconsistency that will always have a final ugliness if left unattended to, even on the best team.

The reality of having Tom Coughlin as their coach is a critical factor in any following sequence. His record prior to becoming the Giant's coach without the approval of the General Manager is in itself unique. It is also interesting, particularly considering the mediocrity of his record.

The journey has been long from the earliest beginnings of professional football to now. A seemingly very good person and a definitely good coach, Tom Coughlin has been around a very long time. People have been known to age well.

Football is a "prime" time sport played by athletes in their prime health for their prime career's success. The Coach is the dictator who decides who sits and who plays, who goes and who stays. The Coach can wreck or seriously undermine careers and motivation. He can choose plays that will end a career or life. He can stock the league with great players that he discards or doesn't like,. all to the detriment of his team, players and fans.

He, Tom Coughlin is the only professional coach that Eli Manning has ever had. The abundance of gifted athletes that has passed through the Giant roster in this time period is approaching legend. The team now lists like a potential "all-star" team. The Giants will be winners. The cost could be more than we as Giant fans want to pay.

Coach Coughlin has been the only professional coach for many players and those players and we are grateful for his service. He is making good decisions but they are clearly not prime decisions. He is not in the prime time of his life.

I am suspicious of Coaches playing the injured to their detriment. I am suspicious of Coaches exposing the "franchise "players in a reckless way. I am suspicious of Giant discards stocking the rest of the league while we play inconsistent football

Eli and the other young greats deserve an opportunity to continue their careers with a fresh and progressive staff, now, and most importantly, achieve the immortality of their time  not his.

A Coach clearly in his prime that which is demonstrated through his actions and decisions would be more in concert with the dynasty that is in progress....

Tom's extended prime? I am suspicious....

# Election 2012... the Postmortem of the GOP

December 4th, 2012

The election is over. A confirmation of the progress of the Obama administration choices, their policy applications and their future plans won a resounding victory over those offered by the opposition in the voting booth on 6 November 2012.

At that time, it was certainly obvious to me that victory was clearly for the Democrats and some hope did remain for the members of the deceased party to accept reality. That was not to be  yet.

The posturing and continued utterances from the deceased party is still, amazingly enough, being heard. The issues are even being repeated as if they had any credibility. Having saturated the media with lies and assorted distractions, the family of this now decomposing creature is offering threats and turmoil to keep the rich from paying more taxes.

The inability to accept reality will persist or continue as long as it is tolerated. The personality conflicts in Congress are entrenched in our nation's history and as long as some remnants of the past decadence is unpunished, the Bush/Cheney horrors to be specific, we will be subjected to these painful reminders.

This last election and the 2008 election marked a visible change in the leadership of the free world, no pun intended. The victory was not Barack over Mitt, nor Democrats over Republicans but cause and social issues from the earliest of human history progressing and getting roots in the future.

This was a victory for accumulated efforts and failures. This result has reassured that all men being accepted and valued by their character and way of life is the standard.

This victory has offered the premise again that war is not a solution ever. Weapon growths, arsenals that clearly cannot be used are being reduced and when discussion and reasoning is possible, all wonders in peace and harmony are also.

This victory increases the probability that, we the people, will be able to share in the best that life offers with increased opportunities and fair play.

This election victory underlines the fact that the future of all life being taken seriously is a not just a dream in progress but an enforced reality. There will be New Gun Control laws.

This victory has endorsed the realization that healthcare will be a possibility for everyone. It has ascertained the fact that Education reform and continued support has been insured.

This victory has insured the immigration rights and dreams of all humanity to a possible fulfillment in this the greatest nation on earth.

This election victory begins the premise of rebuilding the infrastructure and providing jobs with pay. All of this is a possibility because of the results from our sterling democratic efforts and loyalty to our causes.

I am more than ever proud to be a citizen of the USA.

This monumental victory illuminates the false hoods of entitlements, nepotism, voter manipulation and fraud. Above all it rejects racism and bigotry and further ensures the freedoms of women and the less fortunate.

Those tragic character traits will be entombed with the GOP.

Posted in Local, National, News, Parenting, Politics, Social Interests, World | No Comments »

# The Long life of the Serial Killer. Our lives at Risk

December 17th, 2012

Mass murder, homicides, assassination, manslaughter. How long will we continue to allow these threats to our very lives are tolerated? This absolute evil has surfaced again in Newtown. The horrifying magnitude of these events stagger every thought, plan, dream.

In acts far away in Norway or Africa or Palestine we are a bit reserved with our agony and pain. Of course, all children and people, friends and neighbors we know count? Could it just be the incredible shock of early childhood children being slaughtered in mass in their neighborhood school? The count is ongoing....

The tragedy and endless sorrow of these unnecessary deaths has never been enough of a deterrent. Killing evidently justifies more killing. Is it possible that "No Killing" of any kind, for any reason... might start a trend in that direction? Yes, that is what I am saying. Stop the killing!

How naive is that? That would be a great start for all humans. We must simply try. There is no other option and meanwhile we can control the tools of killing.

Being a human and knowing how imperfect we all are, I will concede that there will always be some really sick and dangerous people who would make the victim count always possible. Exploring and studying the youth or past life of the lowest and depraved will not bring any end to the killing or life of the killer. Discussing the credits and minuses of the demented society and family influences are interesting exercises in psychology but fruitless in producing a solution to ending the carnage. Our efforts to find some rational or solace in human behavior is only ego massage/ consolation.

People are unpredictable.

Guns, Rifles, Pistols are not. When loaded with ammunition and in the hands of an irresponsible "person," tragedy happens... Death is often the preferred result when compared to some physical and neurological victims.

All GUNS must be controlled. Eventually, guns can be erased, eliminated. This is the serial killer.

This serial killer has many names. All are sickeningly familiar. Colt, Glock, Sauer, Browning, Beretta, Remington. The most low and depraved life of humanity are empowered by possession of these "killers."

The senseless murders of children in schools, innocents shopping or strolling in the neighborhood, theaters, houses of worship, are becoming legends of infamy. These acts must never be tolerated and all who oppose the measures to safeguard the population by controlling weapons should be prosecuted as accessories.

We can monitor those that own legal weapons.

We can monitor all ammunition sold and replaced.

We can structure rigid guidelines to new owners and ban assault and military weapons.

We can repossess and confiscate all weapons that are unregistered or without approved official purpose.

We can monitor the documented behavior eccentrics and arrest recorded criminals active before the tragedy takes place.

These actions can be taken today... now...!

A serious and effective beginning is absolutely mandated today so we can say we have taken some measures to end this madness.

We can end the life of this "serial killer."

Posted in Local, National, News, Politics, Social Interests, World | No Comments »

# The Coach in NFL Football...

December 27th, 2012

This is an attempt to collect a debt.

As a fan, I do believe that ownership owes a sincere committed effort to produce the best team possible. Incompetence and mediocrity should never be tolerated much less accepted. Ownership should demand the best from every level of the organization.

A football team begins with the choice of "Coach."

Every year teams change coaches. The criteria for the successor or "new" coach is up to imagination often but the change is made because the incumbent staff is unsuccessful at winning.

The winning Coach must be an excellent communicator, a teacher, a confidant for the players and staff. He must also be confident in his ability to choose players and strategy successfully. Mediocre players can win with a skilled effective coach. Gifted players under the stewardship of skilled coaches create dynasties.

These are some examples of excellent coaches. They are also available, now, for the right salary.

Jimmy Johnson... former coach of Cowboys. Now TV analyst

Tony Dungy.... former coach of Colts... Now TV analyst

Bill Cowher.... former coach of Steelers... Now TV analyst...

These men were winning coaches and all exhibited the above-mentioned skills necessary to bring the best from their player's abilities. The skilled players of the Giants were perhaps comparable to Jimmy's Dallas winners but now these new Giants have more gifted athletes.

Bill Belichick, Mike Shanahan, John Fox have never ever had the herd of gifted athletes that Coughlin has abused.

Tom Coughlin of the N.Y. Giants is truly mediocre at best, considering his won-lost record. Yet, he is being considered for immortality? Maybe not! Two Super Bowls in nine years of roller coaster games with a constant injury handicap. This is always followed with the exodus of great players that the league competes with each other to sign and replace their starters! He never takes the ownership of this constant disappointment. He blames players and assistant's. Tom Coughlin is deft at eluding accountability.

Victor Cruz sat the season with the team having receiver shortages because of the Coach's ill decisions.

David Wilson sits his rookie season because the coach plays a severely injured martyr. He actually allowed the team to spend time and money on the runner scrap heap before he would support this gifted athlete drafted in the first round. Surely, a injury suit for the Giants will follow at the end of the veteran runner's career.

Eli Manning's guardian angel is exhausted.

Tom Coughlin is the only problem with the NY Giants. Why he is without criticism baffles me. He needed Steve Spagnola's defense to save his season and then, with acts of God prevailing all over, defeated the Patriots in 2008.

His defensive coordinators must rescue his pathetic offense decisions constantly. Special team's successes are thrown away with impunity because of the blunder choices that follow. Last year he stumbles through the season and his superior athletes rescue him again.

Now we must lose athletes and keep Tom Coughlin. That is the most expensive and demoralizing proposition I can imagine.

He is obviously not retiring and his coaching skills are a myth. Certainly, the neglect of premier draft choices and playing injured players are an infringement on the human resources. This has to be annoying and frustrating for the General Manager.

Media blurts and ownership quotes are all one gets about Tom Coughlin. He is not Jerry Reese's choice for coach now or ever rest assured. This must be addressed by ownership for progress to begin with winning consecutively.

The athletes on the Giants roster are extraordinary every year. They are the result of the superb draft and free agent successes of the personnel acquisition group headed by General Manager Jerry Reese.

When will the General Manager of the NY Giants get the opportunity to choose his selection to Coach?

Posted in Health, News, Politics, Social Interests, Sports, World | No Comments »

# Eavesdroppin on the Wino and Junkie...Say what?

December 31st, 2012

W: wake up? Wake up? You would be dead if it wasn't for droolin....

J: I was just nodding.... thank you.... that is not allowed or against the law     ?

W: Missed you.... heh-heh.... What do you think was a better choice... Palin or Ryan?

J: Are you effing kidding me?

W: C'mon... be nice... he was just a product of that Republican house of rep....

J: Be nice? That "Republican" faction is hopeless.... They just do not want to know the truth or the fact that their conservative label is now clearly a code word for BIGOT.

W: Hmmmmm... you junkies have some hell fire thoughts!

J:... After being stripped of their camouflage by time and historical truth they have to revise the stories of the south.

W: .... You mean the phony stories about being humane while realizing new depths in the deplorable trade of slavery and conducting genocide against the native American?

J: Yes. this last election and the conditions that preceded it dictated a confrontation with reality.... Years of lies and just extraordinary bullshit from the Pilgrims to the "Fiscal Cliff" responsibility of now and they are simply void of honesty, integrity and enough compassion for others....

W: Too harsh man, too harsh.... all Republicans?. America, the beautiful? No compassion?

J: I am not inventing anything here…This congress will go down with the ship because their causes are the ultimate harsh…manipulation and exploitation of "others" for their own selfish gain, and an inability to accept the fact that the "we are the only worthy people on the planet" concept is a cruel lie now and always was.

W: you mean the AntiBama bigotry and the lies they have lived for eternity are linked to the fiscal crisis?

J: Absolutely… and… they obstruct everything that denotes forward progress….

W: I can see your thinking and I like it…. By the way.. I got the tremors last night and fell down just standing up… who is your medicine man?….

Posted in Local, National, News, Parenting, Politics, Social Interests, World | No Comments »

# Khafis... The Prison System

January 10th, 2013

Rahway in 1977 was the same as it was when conceived in prehistoric times.

Dark, labyrinth like, with steel and concrete seasoned with brick and stone, it squatted for all to see. A bird feces green dome sat over the central complex. The second maximum prison in New Jersey until the middle 20th century, it had a green toad effect as it sat by old US highway #1.

The dungeon was actually constructed to warehouse 750 humans in the 19th century. Seventy-seven was the year the population was at an angry overflow of 1200.

No, Rahway wasn't ever big. Certainly, not by today's standards and being totally without a tad of technology or modern creature comforts was a redundant confirmation. It was an old joint with walls that sweat in the summer and the sardine packed population constantly fueled volatile climates and random violence.

Seems it was a hot year from the early spring sentencing. Some inmates were upset when Elvis died. Some. A lot of people die in prison every day. The celebrities outside get a little fame for a few... minutes... People die in prisons much more than one can imagine. Not exactly needed information, perhaps Khafis was an inmate there then and so was Omar, at least that was what the inmates decided fit him more often than Buddha. Both were often the preference rather than a birth or slave name. Often the label was a nickname that might prevail but in the Iron house, you even got your "number" called a few times every day... dehumanizing was easy to feel.

Muslim influence was strong. Before Malcolm X and forward to now that plantation last name and the oddly spelled first English names of African-Americans had an uncomfortable odor  for some us for sure.

The opportunity to embrace Islamic attributes were felt intensely after being submerged in the vat of human misery that is a prison. Other "benefits "from being incarcerated there and then was OJT on survival tactics. from running to striking first.

Discussions on how to be a better "stick-up man" were always enlightening. Did you ever consider what was more intimidating or persuasive during a robbery between a deuce barrel shotgun over and under or side by side? Hmm?

Those Muslim names are common now. In the 3 million inmate population of this civilized and progressive country of which 2.8 million are.... nonwhite, these names flourish. They are often statements of respect from others or of self-value.

This is how Khafis evolved and Omar was initiated. This was Omar's first bid... in Rahway but Khafis had been a product of the NJ correctional system from his early youth. The usual progression was Jamesburg (youth) 2 terms, then Annandale Reformatory (teen) 2 terms followed by Bordentown Reformatory and the PRISON SYSTEM.

Khafis was one of an endless line of life's early ineligibles. Since the beginning of the ghettos in the industrialized cities in every state this process in self elimination was encouraged. Many of these young people were deemed "ineligible "for the rest of their life from the first arrest.

Khafis and Omar met operating the morning dishwasher in the Old Soldiers Home in Edison. Being on minimum custody after serving in max behind the wall was huge. It was also a totally better environment to receive your visits. Omar always got his and Khafis like so many others never got a visit. Some people could even get a "conjugal" visit on the sneak depending on their risk factors.

Great artists, writers, musicians, teachers, scientists, were sprinkled often among the drug felons, B&E craftsmen and assorted serious outlaws. The drug related sentences were so great in quantity and variety we both always knew that the book rules were stacked against people who just wanted their preferred medicine. Everyone from informers to rehab. None of that works and the prison population would be so much less with effective drug laws and separation from the career criminals and psychopaths.

Hell, it was prison. They were not having a bitching session. That was what goes down in "Prison" and/or who is being housed by the taxpayer to the tune of Thirty thousand dollars per year for each.... inmate!!?

My question after getting there is what does one do after being released... Options were and still are short. Dying there is a choice or strong possibility until. paroled and then being deemed "expendable" for life returning to crime and then back to prison?

What does a humane society do with over three million prisoners in the house? What do you when you have to 'release" these often-intelligent angry people? People who have families and human needs like all others yet cannot be included ever again. They are felons or convicts, educated and newly skilled in the courses that you cannot help but remember when "expendable."

Omar said what made Khafis memorable was his fierce pride and strength and heart. A soul commitment to Islam coupled with the fact that he was sticking up a supermarket when his Mom walked in.... She was a breath from fainting as he demanded the store manager give the shaky lady his coat because they all had to go to the freezer etc.

Khafis was not his birth name either.

Posted in Health, National, News, Parenting, Politics, Social Interests | No Comments »

# Justice? For All!

January 18th, 2013

There are a host of crimes that a person can be prosecuted for. The one crime that reigns supreme to me is the liar. I am sure very few humans have not been guilty of this demeaning and completely foolish act that manages to be never forgiven when the perpetrator is caught or uncovered.

When committed in public or under oath, the penalty is scorn, and imprisonment. Absolutely deserving beyond a doubt, this action provides some satisfaction for society but a smidgen of conscience would never free the pathetic soul that must live forever with the label and reputation of the pariah.

Society and the Federal government have zero tolerance of this crime from celebrities and professional athletes and the defenseless minorities. Barry Bonds, Roger Clemens, Lance Armstrong and many others like them all have been pursued relentlessly by the government. While spending millions of the taxpayer's money on prosecuting these self-destructive family felons, the public insists on taking everything from these people including their money, self- respect, freedom and testicles.

The lack of any prosecution efforts on George W. Bush, Dick "Halliburton"Cheney, John Ashcroft and a broad range of Republican /Democratic congressmen during "Dubya's"2000-2008 administration clearly suggests, at least until this point, a double standard.

This omission by the present administration has baffled me since 2008. The freedom, justice and equality mantra mandates indictments and prosecutions for the lies that killed and wounded over 100 thousand American service personnel, destroyed a historically significant nation (Iraq) pillaging and plundering with every step. These vile and unbelievably numerous acts make the cliché "compounding the felony" a reality that threatens everyone.

Their names are just too many to list but the congressman that was having private personal ships built from taxpayer's Federal Defense contracts is an easily retrieved example, to say little about the "weapons of mass destruction" fiasco.

These criminal acts are documented in every way imaginable so I do not understand why these heartless, selfish enemies of peace and equality are left without being held accountable. This delay in prosecution has spawned the venom and lies that persists about the present administration and gave birth to the "Tea Party." It has also provided the gallows as an end for the GOP, sealed their doom as the present party is imaged.

My Dad, a dyslexic before it was presently defined, hated to be lied to. I remember his chastisement when he caught me lying. After enduring "my penalty" for lying to him he sat me on his lap, wiped the tears from eyes and asked me to choose which was the worst between a cold heart thief, a murderer, or a liar.

He didn't wait for my long thought of answer. Perhaps seriously impatient as I often am, he simply said "the Liar" because he could be all three.

Posted in Health, Local, National, News, Parenting, Politics, Social Interests, Sports, World | No Comments »

# The Giants. In Quiet Crises

April 5th, 2013

One year ago, the Giant fans were celebrating a most miraculous recovery. The season had presented the unusual and stunning victories needed to overcome the curious plays and choices of Tom Coughlin.

This has been a year of disappointment from the beginning. All Giant fans know of the annual collapse that comes with Tom Coughlin. This year has brought that collapse and misuse then loss of the usual excellent and gifted players recruited and signed by the "genius" General Manager Jerry Reese.

Mario Manningham, Brandon Jacobs and others followed the annual exodus created by the alignment that supports this alien coach. This alliance has little resemblance to the logic of the general manager. This coach is not the choice of Jerry Reese.

Tom Coughlin has managed to use the players and choices of free agency and draft to produce a most disappointing mediocre winning percentage. The last half of the season going for dung.

He has managed to produce two championship seasons only with the help of newly hired rescue defensive coordinators. How in the hell can he be considered a hall of fame coach or why should that be a thought?

Why can't Jerry Reese have a coach that he selects like other NFL general managers? I am hearing that Mr. Reese, Eli Manning, the team and the fans are stuck with Tom Coughlin until he retires.

Coughlin has managed to unnerve the fans with his inconsistency. This surely causes discomfort among the staff and players. He has managed to isolate and provide an atmosphere of toxicity for Mr. Reese to choose to stay or leave for a more supportive owner.

The contract of Victor Cruz is a familiar scenario since Terrible Tom has been on board. In this example it became glaringly apparent and with other players before this contract that for some reason Mr. Mara speaks when other GMs would be the information source.

The Giants have lost a major assistant to Mr. Reese to another team. The media and again the Giant ownership seem to be limiting the choices and decisions of the General Manager. Surely this is having a negative effect on Mr. Reese. Is it possible Tom Coughlin wants Mr. Reese's job? That would surely sink the Giants for the future.

Briefly, a short review of the facts since Coughlin has been coaching the Giants.

Alienation of major role players from the beginning accompanied by inconsistent winning. The list began with Strahan, Tiki Barber and continued with assorted other stalwarts at their positions. The latest loss to the Giants is Osi Umeniyora. The key factor being most of them leave and are replaced only to start or play for other teams. They all shared one factor in common. A conflict with Tom Coughlin centering on length of playing time and situation.

He has now started the dismantling of a Championship team because he cannot provide the leadership and human awareness to utilize the players.

Victor Cruz is the same sensational player who after catching passes with one hand in his first preseason game had to sit out the season because the Coach did not think he would be needed. He abused Brandon Jacobs psychologically by not playing him. He is doing the same thing to the Giants number one draft choice of last year, David Wilson.

The faults or errors that Tom Coughlin is habitually prone to making are legendary, especially with the coaches that regularly use him as a doormat.

What is glaring here is the fact that he is still the coach? Mr. Mara is often referenced as a source of information instead of the general manager, Jerry Reese.

Tom Coughlin has not ever won constantly and the Giants have been burdened under his pedestrian leadership.

The Giants, my favorite NFL team, are in a period of reorganization now because of retaining Tom Coughlin. The current players are all in a state of flux because of this coach. There are options . . . still. There are other coaches.

When the owners, Mara and Tisch, decide to give the reins to the General Manager, Jerry Reese, the Giants will be moving forward and surely winning consistently.

Posted in Health, Local, National, News, Parenting, Social Interests, Sports, World | No Comments »

# Eavesdoppin' on the Wino and the Junkie...

April 5th, 2013

W: We meet again? Cannot believe it is you?

J: Here we go again... of course it is me... that juice is making your brain so soggy... not a good thing in case you were wondering.

W: Live and let live... try that!

J: You are just the man I wanted to see... I gotta a game for discussion I'd like to play. I say the name or subject and you give your first thought. Then we can reverse,.... know what I'm sayin'?

W: Uh-Oh... go ahead??

J: Bush.

W: Which one?

J: Good question but Dubya. W: Used him like toilet tissue. W: Palin.

J: She looked good... even to John McCain.

W: Cheney.

J: War criminal and liar extraordinaire. J: Condoleeza Rice.

W: Sooo hot and soo smart... a Scorpio too... nobody wanted to hit it.

J: Damn... extra research here.... Hmmmm... you been to see my medicine man?

W: Trump.

J: Confirmation that Money cannot buy Brains or even sincere advisors.

W: Wow... your medicine is the bomb. J: Romney.

W: Same as Trump with more morals but not a lot more... I guess. J: McCain.

W: A weak sacrifice... didn't have a chance... did he do anything... ever? J: Tea Party.

W: Republican Cancer.

J: What do they all have in common?

W: Republicans? Losers? Take your pick. W: GOP.

J: A deceased political party that succumbed to ample quantities of decadent Socio-Economic and Cultural habits mated with genetic descendants of The Oglethorpe colony  Messy too with that internal cannibalization on display.

Posted in Health, Local, National, News, Politics, Social Interests, World | No Comments »

# Boxing....The Manly Art of Self Defense

April 5th, 2013

My favorite sport was Boxing. I was taught and coached with the early skills of offense and defense as a child. The dance of foot movement, the jab, the bob and weave. I loved it.

As a child getting hit did not resonate at all like it began to with age and bigger opponents. I did not like to be hit. I began to reason that a Boxing career would not be a good thing for me. Being very clear about that fact did not stop me from loving the sport.

My childhood heroes were rife with Boxers of all weights and styles. The names will never be forgotten because their signatures were signed in their very blood and underlined with their human sacrifice. Brutally fascinating always, the battles in the arenas by these modern-day gladiators remain statements of human dedication and courage beyond any imagination for all time.

Watching the bouts with fascination and amazement began to change to anticipation of a chilling reality. My adulthood brought the understanding that the art of self-defense left most of its participants with a certain horrific fate, certainly an overwhelming majority. A consistency that still staggers the core of being human, at least, my core.

Blood, guts and disfigurement were always a side product of the fight. The amount of each was the only unknown. Did I really enjoy watching a "fight"? Is my stomach getting weak with age? The pleasure derived from watching a fake or parry followed by a counter punch that breaks a contestant's nose was waning. The blood and the instant lack of balance being an inspiration to the crowd and opponent had a chill to it.

Was this the thrill? Was anticipating the knockout and total separation from senses being as good as it gets? Was the goal actually to.... kill... rather than death just being an occupational hazard? Emile Griffith vs. Benny "Kid" Paret will always come to mind.

Some pugilists manage to escape the disfigurement and dementia that escalates rapidly as they age. However, they do not get a pass on losing a certain sense of self. It matters not whether they were the purest of dedication to their craft. The erosion that follows being understood as another "occupational hazard" is available to all.

The roll call of Boxing's greatest legends is the same listing for tragic deaths and unending sadness in the lives that fade away as we the fan and the public watch.

This addiction to witnessing pain being inflicted on others seems to be a constant in contact sports. Football, the NFL, in particular, has had its flurry of "victims" due to concussion and deliberate impact to cause injury. Millions of spectators watch every week, every event all identifying with the winner... perhaps?

My favorite sport has competition lately. Tennis and Chess have grown. Yet, Boxing and Football still happen to be a joy for me too. I am sure that this all could be a part of the battle between "good and evil" that rages in all of us. As the old Native American said "the winner will be the one who is fed the most."

I like to think I feed the "good" but, my human imperfections are many.

# We are the Family of the future....

Sunday, July 21st, 2013

Interracial families are defined often with scorn and some derision. Mulatto children are black and white, Asian and white is. something else  The naming game can continue and is usually defined by geographical boundaries or some religious reference. Unfortunately, that all leads to a separate biased thinking. We all know those thoughts encompass a myriad of threats to our personal very life, liberty and any possible happiness.

The difficulty that human beings have in accepting each other due to skin color, physical differences, religious or life choices can easily be traced to our human limitations and lack of any technology except the wheel, lever and other simple tools of early human existence as one factor, my opinion only, of course.

The fact that humans were and are eaten like other eatable animals is a subject for another day but we human beings are still capable of the most horrific and dastardly antisocial behavior. We have obviously made progress in our twenty million estimated years of existence on our beloved planet Earth. We are, nevertheless, arrogant beyond belief as a group and so full of our individual selves that our biggest threat is Ego Obesity.

It, EO, is a unfortunate obstacle, but it is obviously going to live on. What is important from my view point is that the beginning and history is there for all to refer to and perhaps understand that separation of humans for the racial and religious or differences in life choices is not only painfully stupid but extremely costly in human lives and material(money?) losses.

Technology...has become high.... er. The vehicles of transportation have continued to evolve or grow and expand.... Bicycle and Rickshaw to Motor driven cycles and cars of all sizes. The Horse is sometimes allowed to be a loved member of the house as a pet... only. Boats from canoes to cruise ships that would shame the "Titanic" and.... Air travel. Fuhgedaboutit.

More Tech or High..er technology  drums to iPad or whatever!!!!

Do you think if humans could access each other for any of the 20 million earlier years as they can now or only the last 150 years . . . . that the "obstacles," and blind stupidity coupled to an unbelievable stubbornness and terminal resistance to progress could ever be as popular?

I doubt it... we learn from our mistakes! That is why we continue to live and other life species does not!

All of this social discomfort of today has its roots or beginnings.... in the "dark ages". no pun here. Life is time to many of us and changes over time have been continuous in our collective human life. Our growth must be, sooner or later, represented in our actions.

Without our growth we could not have reached this clarity or accumulated this level of knowledge.... so we are... truly progressing... growing  socially. Our individual human life is short but collective life is continuing.

Perhaps, in the future people will not be amazed by the color, or ethnicity, or trivial borderlines of origin of a individual, super athlete, or celebrity  because those barriers to free thinking and unconditional acceptance will be history.

Yes, we have been the product of mixed, hopefully hot sexual activity for the longest... we all have mixed DNA. (hi-tech at work) only anti-science people have trouble with this stunning new.... tool?

Skin color is morphing... We will all be a healthy... beige... in the future! just joking?

I seriously think it is totally possible, not necessarily the "beige" or how insignificant can color be?

Yes, in fact, we will be better in every way and our social harmony will be the most pleasurable because.... because we are humans and we learn from our mistakes....

# America.  Unfinished Business

Sunday, July 21st, 2013

There are times and issues that are most difficult to endure. Individually addressed, I am sure these two subjects, times and issues, would have different priorities.

These times and these issues of today affect us all. The absence of addressing or confronting them has not only prolonged our agony but created the burden of spawning countless other problems.

Addressing the issue at hand is the unfinished business of burying the dead. The "dead" being the deplorable group of misinformed apparitions that was formerly known as the Republican party or GOP.

History is a reference that is often distorted by the retriever of said information. We must now give some attention to the history of the Republican party. The spirit of Lincoln was not ever shared or embraced. We have as an everlasting memory the great depression of the thirties and the racism and elitism of that period.

The lack of consideration or ever caring about the common man was common and many were supporters of the Third Reich. The ability to be warmongers and pawns of the wealthy and the lobbyist are confirmed by their representatives and their actions beyond any doubt. My grandfather always said the Republicans were for the rich or wealthy and Democrats for the worker.

Being Afro-American was a disqualifying factor in his mind because" neither party would change our plight or be inclusive of our needs." He still treasured his voting rights and insisted on family commitment to this American privilege.

In this particular issue at this time, we are being obstructed and burdened by this now deceased Republican party. These are people consumed by the social and economic ills of the past who are incapable of being progressive or ever open to the changes that have become a integral part of today's society. The Republicans, new or old, are STILL a group of misinformed prevaricators who have no intention of facing their crimes and social ills.

The ideas and proposals from this group are a sad reminder daily of their terminal constipation. The attempts to be pious via Bible based or so-called Conservative dogma is insensitivity at its best. They are also unabashed liars and total hypocrites. Unfortunately, that often can be said of many "politicians" in general but we are focusing on this time, our time in history and the social diseases that are fostering hate, discord and death to the masses.

The "life after death" group called the GOP or "Tea Party" has embraced and tried with every effort to retard and obstruct any plan or proposal from the now twice elected administration in the United States or the will of the people for five years.

Let's briefly list their latest blunders.  sequester, fiscal cliff, use of congressional rules for personal or special interests. They are panderers to all issues that may be an obstacle to approval of the present administration actions without any thought of the citizens and other humans of the world.

Spending taxpayer money and vital time with impunity in search of a reason to discount the first administration in U.S. history to be so effective in Foreign Affairs and Diplomacy, vibrant growing economy and ending unemployment is beyond redemption. Their list of insults, stupidity, and crimes is very long from my point of view. This fuels my curiosity about "unfinished business." Why these people have not been held accountable baffles the hell out of me.

They are committed to insulting women and being opportunistic bigots. Praying for the collapse or failure of Obamacare they march in dysfunctional goose step backwards embracing decadence and unbelievable resistance to accepting the failures and absurdity of their present positions.

These so-called pro-lifers and stalwarts of human decency would STILL allow misfits and the mentally deranged to access weapons that are designed for killing masses of human beings. after Aurora,

Newtown and the daily senseless murders in our homes and neighborhoods.

Trayvon Martin is another "expendable" victim in an endless line before him who is a casualty of this horrible mental disorder that my country has condemned most other nations for, most, but in their hypocrisy, condone or even harbor and nurture and defend that same insulting and dehumanizing thinking.

Not one "Republican Leader" has supported the right of Trayvon to stand his ground or questioned the absurd racist laws of Florida and the States of the Confederacy or other states that has used "stand your ground laws" to kill minorities.

These still "active" social misfits have found strength in not being held accountable for their past crimes and total obstructive behavior in trying to resist the progress in human growth and brotherhood.

Now, "they" are holding on to Benghazi and the fact that the IRS has "focused" on their element while that farcical attempt to hijack the last presidential election with their money manipulations revealed they never had a chance to win legally. Anything to distract from the progress of this nation under new leadership from the top down. Anything.

The DOJ is snooping ? Hmmm. Atty. General Holder has got to be "champing on the bit" in his eagerness to present indictments. He can certainly start with Bush, Cheney, Rumsfeld etc. It would take more space and more time than I have to extend this perpetrator list. However, this is the most necessary "Business" to finish on this planet. There must be JUSTICE,. NOW!

These pawns and their petty harassing hemorrhoid moves that are funded by the illegally wealthy will disappear faster than Al-Qaida.... IF Mr. Holder opens inquiry and sticks an indictment or two in the mix. This is a promised fact, no crystal ball needed!

These are not ordinary times and this administration is anything but "ordinary." A most needed change was implemented and executed by a most needed administration. This is the most "NEEDED" indictment.

We must demand accountability and justice for the history of mankind. The crimes of the Bush administration, local, national and world combined all the worst scenarios in the history of mankind or politics.

There is no reason to prolong mandating accountability. These social predators will never admit their crimes or acknowledge the progress since their removal from power. They will never admit that all humanity deserves equality or that the Affordable Care Act.... (Obamacare?) is a success and a growing strength and blessing to the needy. They will never admit the economy, including jobs, is better and growing more than ever before in U.S. history. The Dow Jones index is approaching 16k. They will never admit that segregation is a detriment in every way to human harmony. Their hypocritical, racist, elitist legal maneuvers are in fact a cover for more sinister possibilities, if that can be imagined.

These "Republicans" have fostered all of the problems we now are distressed and threatened by... All are Republican based. The most egregious factor about them is their constant distortion of the truth or they believe their ridiculous gutless lies to avoid accountability.

They promised doom and chaos from everything they couldn't obstruct. None of this was ever truth as is the rest of their reasoning or rational. The only common factors are the bigotry and racism mated with inhuman feelings for minorities and any dissenter.

There is no mystery here. These people are the former leaders of the Republican party  The wars, the recession, inner house dissension, unemployment and lack of a positive plan are their signatures. How in hell can we listen to people like John McCain, Sarah Palin and the "tea party"? Why should we consider these people who have no history of being positive or accurate in their thinking or planning and have all supported the sick and absolutely criminal actions of the past administration?

Why anyone can possibly respect or trust these social misfits, proven liars in ANY WAY is an astounding curiosity forever unless it is just the remaining scent from their ghost toilet use that will surely vanish with the ventilation of indictments.

# My Giants.... 2013....

Monday, September 23rd, 2013

The New York Giants again have the most impressive athletes in the NFL.

Jerry Reese is the General manager who has to accept this coach that has absolutely made every season of his tenure a nerve-wracking experience and then, again, had to replace the roster losses with an equal or superior player.

Now he must continue to endure the incredibly curious "offensive" decisions of "Terrible Tom Coughlin"!

Yes, I said it before and with infinitely more conviction I say it now!... Nice guy, father figure maybe  Loser Coach!

Coughlin is the only "NFL COACH" who would have the ball, 1st and 10 on the 5-yard line in the first pre-season game and choose to pass on first, second, and third downs with a plethora of running backs grinding their teeth with eagerness to blast into the end zone. The result, predictably enough, sets the table for the Giants new season. A field goal. frustration for running backs, disappointment from Quarterbacks and fans.

This again was followed by total undue stress on the defensive component and always the fans.

Typical Coughlin?. Absolutely!

Now we are looking at game #3 of the season after having lost the first 2. We have also lost players through injury and attrition as usual. We must include "braindead" decisions offered as excuses along with player blame.

We have lost any real hope for success for this season. without miracles aplenty. We have lost years of our lives and athlete purity.

We have lost the "fruitful" years of our youth. We have kept Tom Coughlin... Why?

How or what do we the NY Giant fan, player, or management owe Tom Coughlin? Mr. Mara may feel protective about TC and loyalty is fine but loyalty to fans and players come first.

Everyone has to go sooner or later  one way or the other. Why is Tom still here? Your job record or capability of job success usually determines possession of same job. His record, except for miraculous wins including 2 Super Bowls over 10 years absolutely sucks.

His legendary ability to show an infantile loss of control in critical moments is not a compliment or what a recruiter would ask for in a new candidate. It is, however, a most valid negative indicator according to valid medical professionals. His job planning and approach may be understandable but being a "relic" and being "understood" by your opponent is not what a winning team, Army, or player would want.... if a team could be a winner with that obvious handicap.

Which easily explains the results. of the Giant games. The Giants

have players like no other team in the league and Tom doesn't have a clue what to do with them. Losses could be heavy this year. Players cannot be replaced as easily as coaches although good coaches are hard to find...

Other Coaches must be given an opportunity to coach the Giants while we still have a team or other great athletes of today! Our time is now ?

Injuries are mounting.

I have pointed out examples from years past until now  Tom Coughlin is the same old dude from 30 years ago  Everyone and their game has changed profoundly but not Tom.

The hits Eli takes are an insult to his ability be a quarterback. This is due to a total lack of proper planning, strategy, preparation and understanding of today's game. Tom eerily continues to expose Eli to career peril due to this personal flaw and weakness unnecessarily.

Perry Fewell is not Steve Spagnuolo, who saved Tom Coughlin's toasted buns in '07 but being on the same page with your staff helps too, I'd bet.

Now, no one is on the same page as Coughlin obviously, and with a depressing frequency, more and more. Dementia has begun! Yes!

Most importantly, some wonderful athletes have never played for another professional COACH in their NFL careers! Does Eli and Cruz or Hicks and JPP, Tuck only get to be led by Tom Coughlin... That really smells badly.

Really bad the more one breathes... Ugh!

At this time, except for scarcely few moments, Coughlin always blames others. Players have to be destroyed. Teams and fan base get to be decimated while this" senior citizen," whose heritage is totally suspect, gets to blame others for his consistent malfunctions while standing on their careers and futures to embellish his very own mediocre history.

Boxers often don't know when to quit.  too bad they cannot be fired before it is too late?

This extended.... period. is truly adding insult to injury.

He has easily destroyed the careers of a minimum of 30 excellent football players in his 10 years with the Giants (3 py) and six (6) other potentially winning teams.

The players of today need the opportunity to play for another coach.

Any other coach would be held totally accountable, many times over. except Tom Coughlin...

Only Tom Coughlin??? Why not him?.... What!!! Jimmy Johnson for the money, Lou Saban... more money?. Too bad, Pete Carroll is on a roll.... Bill Belichick.  with a 6th rd. draft choice? Tom Brady always sticks in my craw.

Good Coaching wins.... Cowher waits...

# The New President... and New World Participation?

Monday, September 23rd, 2013

Syria, an ancient, significant land and a vital part of the all so very important mid-east, has set the table for the most recent buffet for the world and it's leaders to dine on. The menu was most disturbing although the diners and the Chefs/staff were more than familiar.

The disturbing menu?... Death... served by one of the most horrific killers known to mankind ever. Poison gas... Sarin.... to be specific... Yes, we humans are all killers and we argue about what is "humane" in that process?

Assuming that we all really do want to "stop the "Killing," we all proceed and invest our hopes with that eventual goal.... er  Don't we? Summits, Conferences, Secret agents, Diplomats all want to end the killing.... even Wars are to stop the killing right? Hmmm?

As a veteran of the U.S. Army, Chemical Corps, trained at the Chemical Corps School, Ft. McClellan Ala., my experience with our arsenal of the United States', is first hand.

Although the letters CBR have somehow faded from the use they represented.... Chemical, Biological (germ/bacteria), Radiological (nuclear) warfare... or... how we can kill individuals and masses without guns, etc. about sums it all up except for the cleanup and aftermath.

These methods are totally real and have been for a very long time... Scare stories valid or imagined are not ever a goal here. The fact that these "killers" seemed to be feared notably by all humans should not be taken lightly...

CBR weapons are just other tools of death.

Killing anyone for any reason should be stopped immediately... which sets the table for the buffet in Syria or has the predicted critical moment been resolved... for the moment,. with arch enemy Putin in agreement?

The New President continues to offer new leadership to differ sharply from the past.  What? He kills people too!! Back to the drawing board?. Not quite!

I offer that this monumental effort (stop the killing) must have a declared beginning! This must start somewhere, now, and the effort to eliminate killing must not be ever be halted or stopped. A slow pace for many is unacceptable but a slow pace is better than none. Ask any turtle. Diversions simply must be frustratingly tolerated to persist towards the ultimate goal.

This goal will not be done today or tomorrow but we must simply never ever stop the effort. The effort to end killing or taking life. Humans are a great example of life to begin with.

That said, this President's limitations are as long as most other humans, I am sure. His significant contributions, however, are a challenge for comparison.

The list continues from the beginning of taking office to now... From the financial crises, to the Economy rescue, Industry and Auto salvation, Disaster Maintenance, choice of Judges, Cabinet, Office delegation, Drones and diplomacy. The air and Vibes are different now.

The Wars in Iraq and Afghanistan. saving lives now and in the future, the new leadership here and around the world is responding positively, to this "New U.S." President.

A pact with Russia and China without rattling sabres? Syria relinquishing chemical weapons.?... Really?. New diplomacy and Foreign Relations at work?....

A strange challenge that still remains is working with the terminally backward and deliberately resistant to any progress Conservatives, known as Tea Party/Republican  zombies. They actively do and will continue to persist in their denial of reality.

From Racism to Lack of Gun Control, with senseless murders abounding at home and controlling any one's life that permits, they proceed like no refutation of their pathetic lies and their twisted anti-social practices had ever been presented or questioned. They now actually threaten to disrupt government in an extortion attempt to interrupt health care or Obamacare, which is now federal law of the land.

Unfortunately, these bizarre continuances confirm a offering of multiple mental abnormalities that assuredly threatens all others on many levels.

At some point or at every time opportunity avails itself. these issues and people must be addressed and checked... over and again until their actions are no longer tolerated!

Our freedom, love of same and all that it entails is always at risk when these issues and the people who support these issues are not confronted and held accountable.

# Eavesdoppin' on the Wino and the Junkie... growing

Thursday, September 26th, 2013

'W: Dude! What are u sayin?

J: That Coke is better when you smoke it.... not drink it?.... just a rumor.... hmmmm? Nah?

W: Hey!... that Crack will make you smell bad and destroy your neighborhood image. You might fight your Grandmother, I heard....

J: That "Crack" is fast food, not quite what I was having in mind but in a larger sense... All those "Brain Manipulators" better known as Drugs (illegal and legal), Booze(beer-infinity), have been known to be a partner in some horrific tragedy in human lives,... hitting Grandma.... is truly bad but so is a revolting body odor... or.... the dual standard, hypocritical justice applications.... the real problem. The War on drugs is a fifty-seven-year war with all casualties and victims.

.no winning side?.... Fifty-seven years with the same solution expecting a different result?.... Farm owner or not this is Bull Shit!

W: Huh?

W: Whoa... is... Smelling.... a.horrific tragedy?

J: er.... to me?.... Absolutely... but you are not in that League of stink man, or we couldn't hang... These damn people need to stop lying and do something to change the results for the better... They NEED to legalize a man's medicine too....

W: Speaking of stinking badly, the so-called GOP... Republicans... Conservative…ly speaking, of course... Whoeeeeeeeeeeeee... Damn!... What a hot mess they are!

J: They have no understanding of who they are without the lies, nepotism and bigotry.... Their common factor is racism and suppression of the minorities and have nots... This is not easily done or practiced with all the technological progress of today.

W: Word! That going back to school has got you to sizzle lately... cannot believe you still do drugs....

J: My Medicine?!!... Everyone has their medication.... mine are illegal... sometimes...

W: Speaking of medicine. Reality and truth, like all good medicine, may be hard to take, but clears the air and bowels too... if that is possible at the same time?

J: What are talking about now?

W: The Catholic Church...?... I love that new Pope, man... so real, so empathetic. Finally, a living representative of the thinking that provides the medicine that cures so many human ills. He is awesome man, a Catholic Pope too?

J: True... I cannot even buy into any specific way or faith... but this Pope here... and now? He is clearly a caring, humble and courageous human that I, most importantly, trust... huge for me!

...Most clergy, regardless of faith or sect, I am totally suspicious of This is a wonderful time to be alive!

W: Rumor suggests that Donald Trump was chosen poster child for the GOP and Sarah Palin got tiffed and took her demented fox crew home.

J: Please  Let the dead rest in peace

# Barack Obama... A Chosen President

Wednesday, October 2nd, 2013

Serving with patience, humor and guile, with intelligence and wisdom beyond his earthly years, this president seemed to be waiting for them, Republicans and Democrats, to come to their senses.

Exhibiting daily a certain unbelievable courage this man has done his job as the 44th President of the United States. This is the big job... in my opinion, President of the U.S. Barack Obama was chosen President of the United States United States in 2008 and 2012.

The chaos existing in government and foreign affairs was monumental in 2008. The sick group of politicians that had collapsed the economy with lies, destroyed a culture and a nation while needlessly killing 10 million citizens was so disgusting the leaders could not make appearances for their "new" candidates.

These Republicans have had their deplorable acts documented here and in other media. Nothing can change the acts or the actors. They have spent every opportunity in every way to obstruct and constrict any flow or peace and harmony since losing the election.

Absolutely refusing to function under their elected leader because they are bigots... racists. This "refusal to govern" is NOT about the Affordable Health care Act. Neither was Benghazi, Economy, Unemployment or whatever else those selfish tools of the rich chose to take issue with to disrupt government functions.

Obama represents the same principle of life to "Republicans" that Jesse Owens did to" Nazis." This is not 1936. The Republicans are forever in 1936. Progress is slower with some people than others.

The last five years have exposed these "patriots" for what they have always been. Liars about everything, Racists with elitist and religious hypocrisies running rampant. These are their limitations! This is mental illness. Why is this group of dangerously mentally ill still in office?

Vowing to avoid accepting the truth of facts, vowing to obstruct the will of the people, and then deliberately disrupting the welfare and harmony of all families for their personal insanity. These are their documented actions. It confirms many possible mental disorders of which none.... are... right... Pardon the pun. Certainly, all are wrong for an elected leader or a mere social citizen.

Mr. President, I ask is there any reason we cannot request Mr. Holder to present some indictments now?

He has a plethora of choices. These people are the same liars from the Bush support group, all of them. Any few will be enough for any reason.

The people who are financing these amoeba minded tea party conservatives Republicans have to be addressed.

Shutting down the government?

Preceded by threats to do this . . . unless a "fee" is rendered or a law is changed. Deliberately compromising individual and national security? Initiating the threat of economic disaster?

Is seeding anarchists illegal?

To play insidious games with the psyche of every man, woman and child. This, again, truly is a moral crime.

It will never be addressed without the accountability that will come with indictments.

Your delay in asking for specific acts to be investigated has ceased to have reason if there could ever be a reason.

My life as an only child of an African-American couple in North New Jersey held many memories. Mostly pleasant, I was raised with a special love and pride in my country.

An Army veteran and family man, my early adulthood was centered on surviving the conflicts I had with the limitations to my freedom and the injustices encountered along my way.

Civil rights activist, Ass't Reg. Training Officer for N.J. Head Start Program, Purchasing Agent, my experiences included the undeniable reality of American Democracy being another work in progress. This was a crushing disappointment many times over before being accepted as "early growth" pain.

Adjusting to that with many trials and errors as my school, I know now that I am a most fortunate person and if a dedication might seem in order, I would like to dedicate this book to my Mom and beloved family.